THE ENDURING STRUGGLE

George H. Phillips

THE ENDURING STRUGGLE

Indians in California History

series editors:
Norris Hundley, jr.
John A. Schutz

MTL, Inc.

THE ENDURING STRUGGLE:
INDIANS IN CALIFORNIA HISTORY

George Harwood Phillips

© Copyright 1996 by Materials For Today's Learning, Inc.
1575 Linda Way, Sparks, Nevada 89431.
All rights reserved.

© Copyright 1981 by Boyd & Fraser Publishing Company, 3627 Sacramento Street, San Francisco, CA 94118. All rights reserved.

Manufactured in the United States of America.

Library of Congress catalog card number: 81-66060

ISBN 0-929651-18-9

6 7 8 9 . 5 4 3

EDITORS' INTRODUCTION

MENTION THE NAME CALIFORNIA and the popular mind conjures up images of romance and adventure of the sort that prompted the Spaniards in the 1540s to name the locale after a legendary Amazon queen. State of mind no less than geographic entity, California has become a popular image of a wonderful land of easy wealth, better health, pleasant living, and unlimited opportunities. While this has been true for some, for others it has been a land of disillusionment, and for too many it has become a place of crowded cities, congested roadways, smog, noise, racial unrest, and other problems. Still, the romantic image has persisted to make California the most populated state in the Union and the home of more newcomers each year than came during the first three hundred years following discovery by Europeans.

For most of its history California has been shrouded in mystery, better known for its terrain than for its settlers—first the Indians who arrived at least 11,000 years ago and then the Spaniards who followed in 1769. Spaniards, Mexicans, and blacks added only slightly to the non-Indian population until the American conquest of 1846 ushered in an era of unparalleled growth. With the discovery of gold, the building of the transcontinental railroad, and the development of crops and cities, people in massive numbers from all parts of the world began to inhabit the region. Thus California became a land of newcomers where a rich mixture of cultures pervades.

Fact and fiction are intertwined so well into the state's traditions and folklore that they are sometimes difficult to separate. But close scrutiny reveals that the people of California have made many solid contributions in land and water use, conservation of resources, politics, education, transportation, labor organization, literature, architectural styles, and learning to live with people of different cultural and ethnic heritages. These contributions, as well as those instances when Californians performed less admirably, are woven into the design of the Golden

State Series. The volumes in the Series are meant to be suggestive rather than exhaustive, interpretive rather than definitive. They invite the general public, the student, the scholar, and the teacher to read them not only for digested materials from a wide range of recent scholarship, but also for some new insights and ways of perceiving old problems. The Series, we trust, will be only the beginning of each reader's inquiry into the past of a state rich in historical excitement and significant in its impact on the nation.

Norris Hundley, jr.
John A. Schutz

CONTENTS

Introduction   1

1 First Californians   4
  Sociopolitical Organization   5
  Environmental Knowledge   9

2 Intrusion   3
  Initial Contact   14
  Spanish Settlement   17

3 Mission Life   21
  Discontent   22
  Resistance   26

4 **Aftermath**   33
  Economic Integration   34
  Social Readjustment   37

5 New Pressures   42
  Violent Interaction   43
  Negotiations   47

6 Deprivation   53
  Revitalization   54
  Dispossession   57

7 Legalities   62
  Jurisdiction   62
  Termination and Compensation   66

8 Contemporary Scene   71
  Urbanization   72
  Activism   74

  Notes   79
  Suggested Readings   85
  Index   91

Illustrations

Costanoans Fighting a Spanish Soldier, ca. 1791   18
Gambling Game at Mission San Francisco, ca. 1816   24
Mission San Gabriel, 1832   29
Mounted Indian in San Joaquin Valley, 1853   39
Indian Miners at Taylorville, 1849   43
Indian Shacks near San Diego, ca. 1900   59
Removal of the Cupeño, 1902   60

Maps

California Indian Territories circa 1769   7
Missions and Ranchos in California   31
Unratified Treaty Lands in California, 1851–52   51
Indian Reservations and Rancherias in California   68

INTRODUCTION

WHEN DIFFERENT RACIAL, ethnic, or national groups participated in the history of a region, the contributions of each should be carefully evaluated and put into perspective. This is more easily said than done, however, because the intellectual atmosphere at the time of writing often dictates the historian's emphasis and preference. Through the years, California historians have preferred the Spanish to the Mexicans at one time, the Americans to the Spanish at another, but only occasionally have they paid much attention to the Indians. The commonly held notion that the Indian response to the Euro-American intrusion was basically passive and therefore historically unimportant has discouraged research.

This perception of Indian passivity was created not by Euro-Americans who interacted with still-functioning Indian societies but by Anglo-Americans who observed Indians after they had been colonized and demoralized. During the 1870s and 1880s several Indian agents reported on the deplorable moral and physical condition of the Indians in southern California.[1] The two most widely read accounts were written by a famous crusader for Indian reform, Helen Hunt Jackson. One appeared in *Century Magazine* in 1883, the other in the post-1883 editions of her widely read book on the mistreatment of the Indian, *A Century of Dishonor*. In 1884 she also published *Ramona*. A nineteenth-century "tearjerker" of dubious historical or literary merit, the novel contains a colossal cast of cardboard characters, including the near-perfect Ramona, her pure-blooded Indian lover of gentle character and enormous talents, an aristocratic and tyrannical Mexican guardian, a good mission padre, and a collection of ugly, evil gringos.[2] Although the novel and the reports focused national attention on the perilous condition of the state's aboriginal inhabitants, they also stereotyped the California Indian as always needing the assistance of or being seriously harmed by Spaniards, Mexicans, or Americans. This stereotype has increased the difficulty of recognizing the Indians' contribution to California history.

Understanding the Indians' role in California history has also been hindered by the passage of time. Nineteenth-century historians, such as Theodore H. Hittell, Alexander Forbes, and Hubert Howe Bancroft, investigated Indian activity more thoroughly than those of the late twentieth century, probably because they lived during the final phase of Indian independence. Unfortunately, the healthy realism of these historians gave way to a romanticism that elevated the Spanish missionaries to near sainthood and idealized the Mexican rancheros as masters of a life style approaching pastoral perfection. Modern historians have corrected these distortions, but somehow the Indian got lost in the process.

Adding to the difficulty in appreciating the historical worth of the Indian is the way academic disciplines have fragmented the California past. Anthropologists and archaeologists, utilizing material remains and Indian informants, have concentrated on reconstructing Indian cultures as they existed before white contact. Historians, relying almost exclusively on documentary evidence, have investigated the history of the Euro-Americans who produced the documents. Of course, anthropologists have studied the change wrought on Indian societies as a result of white contact; some archaeologists have excavated the ruins of missions, presidios, and ranchos; and a few historians have investigated Indian history. But for the most part historians, anthropologists, and archaeologists have yet to analyze thoroughly Indian activity between initial white contact and final colonization. Those years witnessed the persistence of Indian societies as politically independent and culturally durable units. They also saw important historical events determined not only by the expansion of Euro-American settlements, but also by the interaction of Indians and whites.

Investigating the history of an indigenous people within the geopolitical framework established by intruding peoples, however, presents difficulties. First a Spanish geographical abstraction and presently an American political unit, California lacks natural boundaries and thus never contained a homogeneous Indian population. Even today anthropologists remain divided as to the eastern geographical limits of what they have designated the California culture area. Many Indian groups residing on the eastern side of the Sierra Nevada and the Cascade ranges shared more cultural traits with peoples belonging to the Great Basin, Plateau, and Southwest culture areas than with those occupying the western side of the mountains. Because this study evaluates the Indians' most important contributions to post-contact California history, it is geographically limited to where Indian-white interaction was most intense—the coastal belt, the adjacent inland valleys, and the foothills of the Sierra Nevada. Events taking place on the eastern border are mentioned only briefly.

Whenever possible and appropriate, Indian testimony is presented, but even here problems arise. There is a lack of precision in such testimony about names and dates, and appropriate documents for the early period are quite scarce. But when available and relevant to the discussion at hand, Indian testimony is invaluable because it reveals the hopes, fears, beliefs, and values of a people undergoing profound social, economic, and political change.

First Californians

FOR MANY YEARS anthropologists postulated that mankind had advanced through several socioeconomic stages—from hunting and wild-food collecting, through pastoralism and agriculture to the urban industrial state. From this perspective, those who remained at the hunting and gathering stage were somehow lacking in spirit or intelligence. Indeed, as the theory goes, only when freed from the perpetual insecurity of the hunt were people able to develop complex (and therefore better) material cultures and sociopolitical institutions.

Because much of our information about hunter-gatherers has come from marginal regions of the world, distortions concerning the quality of life experienced by all such peoples have been presented in the ethnographic literature. Often forced into inhospitable areas by intruding Europeans, hunter-gatherers have been observed living at a bare subsistence level. That they once may have occupied fertile lands and lived in relative prosperity has only recently been acknowledged by anthropologists. A few now claim that some hunting and collecting peoples, such as the first Californians, actually maintained a healthier and more varied diet than did many who practiced horticulture or pastoralism.

Sociopolitical Organization

ARCHAEOLOGISTS GENERALLY agree that Asian peoples first migrated into the Western Hemisphere across the Bering Strait from Siberia to Alaska sometime between 50,000 and 20,000 B.C. Following the large game upon which they subsisted, they crossed the strait because at different periods during the Pleistocene epoch, commonly called the Ice Age, a land bridge connected Siberia and Alaska. When glacial ice locked up immense amounts of the planet's ocean water, the bridge appeared; when meltage poured water back into the oceans, the bridge disappeared.

The main route into the present United States was probably along an ice-free corridor that extended from the Arctic Ocean southwards through Canada. From this route, which lay just east of the Rocky Mountains, some groups branched off to the west. By 9,000 B.C., or perhaps much earlier, their descendants had reached the Pacific Coast.

Apparently the first Californians relied heavily on large game for food. This is inferred from the types of projectile points found at camp sites. The weight and size of the points indicate they were hurled by means of the atlatl, or spear thrower. The Indians hunted the bison, horse, sloth, and mammoth, but supplemented their diet with smaller mammals. Grinding implements for processing plants are lacking at the earliest sites, indicating California's first residents were not dependent on vegetal foods.

Between 6,000 and 3,000 B.C., however, Indians diversified their diet by exploiting a variety of plant and marine life. From San Luis Obispo to San Diego counties, archaeologists have uncovered numerous food-grinding implements, such as milling stones and mullers. The food-collecting economy also spread throughout the San Joaquin Valley, the northern Coast Range, and the foothills of the Sierra Nevada. The archaeological record further indicates that by 3,000 B.C. new immigrants had reached the Santa Barbara coast where they exploited the rich marine life, especially shellfish, sea mammals, and fish. About this time the Channel Islands were also occupied. After 3,000 B.C. other economic changes took place. The large number of mortars, pestles, grinding stones, and mullers unearthed along the coastal strip indicates that Indians now relied heavily on the abundant plant life.

Specialized regional cultures, the precursors of those encountered by Europeans in the sixteenth century, had emerged by 2,000 B.C. Members of these regional cultures came to speak as many as eighty distinct languages belonging to no less than five language families—Hokan, Penutian, Uto-Aztecan, Algic, and Na-Dene.

The first people to arrive in California were probably organized into bands. Each band consisted of a few extended families that could work and live together in relative harmony. Membership was voluntary with individuals and families changing allegiance or forming new bands as they wished. Leadership consisted of a headman whose position rested on his hunting prowess. His powers were limited, and he governed with the consent of the adult male members. Although a relatively simple form of organization, the band constituted a type of government since it regulated the public affairs of the entire group—the prime function of all governmental systems. In the band, however, political, economic, and religious undertakings were seldom differentiated. Because of its small size (usually fewer than fifty members) and mobility, the band was ideally suited for a people who hunted large game.

Beginning about 8,000 B.C. and continuing over a long period of time, most of the large animals disappeared. This dramatic change in the ecosystem resulted from an increase in the temperature which thinned out the lush vegetation upon which the animals depended. But the Indians successfully adapted to the environmental changes by increasing their dependence on wild plant foods and small game. This, in turn, led to great population increase. By the time of white contact in 1542, the area between the inland mountains (Cascades and Sierra Nevada) and the coast carried a population of about 310,000.

Population increase contributed to the formation of a new type of sociopolitical organization. Anthropologists postulate that the lineage replaced the band as the basic governmental unit in California sometime after 6,000 B.C. when the population rapidly expanded and when Indians settled in permanent villages. The lineage accommodated a larger membership than

CALIFORNIA INDIAN TERRITORIES Circa 1769

the band and provided a precise set of social rules. Since members traced their descent to a common ancestor, they considered themselves biologically related and thus could not intermarry. Genealogical relationships determined how individuals behaved toward one another.

In 1940 a Pomo well over 100 years of age explained to an anthropologist what kinship meant to Indians.

> Without the family [i.e., lineage] we are nothing, and in the old days before the white people came the family was given the first consideration by anyone who was about to do anything at all. This is why we got along. We had no courts, judges, schools, and the other things you have, but we got along better than you. . . . We were taught to leave people alone. We were taught to consider that other people had to live. We were taught that we would suffer from the devil, spirits, ghosts, or other people if we did not support one another. The family was everything, and no man ever forgot that. Each person was nothing, but as a group joined by blood the individual knew that he would get the support of all his relatives if anything happened.[1]

Whereas band membership was unstable and often changed, lineage membership was permanent except when individuals were ostracized and outsiders incorporated. Both the band and lineage possessed leadership positions occupied by headmen with limited powers. But the lineage headman was surrounded with officers who formed a governing council of staff. Unlike the ad hoc council of the band that met only when necessary and consisted of all adult male members, the lineage council formed a permanent institution with specific and limited membership.

When lineage membership became too large to be governed effectively, factions left to form new lineages. These related lineages shared a common ancestor (the founder of the original lineage) and thus formed a clan. Depending on time and place, the clan was either an organization that occasionally mustered its members for ceremonial, economic, or military purposes or a permanent government superstructure that regulated the affairs of its several lineages.

Along the southern coast, Hokan-speaking Chumash and Uto-Aztecan-speaking Gabrielino developed political systems that superseded the lineage and clan. At the time of white contact, they resided in numerous towns, some containing a thousand persons or more. Town government probably developed as a result of competition among groups over the rich marine resources of the southern coast. Population size and density became so great that a more centralized political unit was required to ensure protection.

How a town conducted its public affairs is open to conjecture. Perhaps a council, consisting of the headmen and elders from the various lineages, carried on the day-to-day business of running the society. Elite lineages were associated with each town, and kinship determined social ranking. Archaeological evidence indicates that Chumash towns were socially stratified and economically differentiated. Members of elite lineages and wealthy individuals, such as canoe owners who had distribution rights to the maritime harvest, constituted an aristocracy.[2]

In regard to size, structure, and economic orientation, Chumash and Gabrielino societies had more in common with the maritime peoples of the Northwest Coast, such as the Tlingit and Kwakiutl, than with other California Indian groups. But whether they developed town governments or remained basically organized by lineage and clan, California Indians maintained relatively stable societies until white contact.

Environmental Knowledge

B Y THE SIXTEENTH century, the Indians of California had acquired considerable knowledge about their environment. They hunted deer, tule elk, Roosevelt elk, and pronghorn antelope as well as small animals, including rabbits, rodents, squirrels, ducks, songbirds, quail, and mice. Bows and arrows, snares, throwing sticks, pitfalls, and nets were employed to kill or capture the game.

Coastal Indians exploited a variety of marine life, such as the king and silver salmon and the steelhead trout. As attested by the numerous shell mounds and bones found at many coastal sites, Indians eagerly sought mollusks and sea mammals. Sea mussel, oyster, scallop, and California venus clam were particularly abundant along the southern coast, and sea mussel, bentnose macoma, and oyster were found along the northern coast. The peoples of the Santa Barbara Channel and nearby islands relied heavily on the sea lion, sea otter, and harbor seal.

On the Sacramento and San Joaquin rivers and their tributaries, fishing was a most rewarding economic activity. The salmon semiannually spawned upstream in great numbers, so a concentrated fishing effort often brought great return. Weirs and traps were placed in streams but only for a limited number of days, thus allowing some of the salmon to pass through to be caught by groups residing upriver. Because political boundaries often encompassed river and stream fronts, inter-lineage disputes were probably frequent as groups vied with one another for preferred fishing territories.

Indians also collected a variety of plant foods, such as the buckeye, sage seed (chia), the epos root, and different kinds of berries. But the acorn was the most important plant staple in California, and Indians ranked in order of preference at least ten species of oak. Indians gathered the acorns in the fall while still on the trees, the harvesting continuing until a winter's supply had been acquired.

The acorn became an essential food staple once Indians mastered the process of grinding the nut into a meal and leaching the tannic acid. Pouring hot water through the meal placed either in a basket or a sand-lined depression in the ground eliminated the poison. The meal was then roasted, baked, or boiled.

So economically important was the acorn that the territory controlled by each society was often determined by the number and productivity of oak trees. Failure of an acorn crop could cause severe hardships, even starvation. Crises of this kind often led to conflicts in which territorial aggrandizement resulted. Those regions containing the most productive oak trees carried the largest populations and were the most contested.

Gaining knowledge of their environment required a persistent effort over a long period and indicates that Indians, contrary to established opinion, were not passive occupants of the land. Rather, they experimented actively in developing techniques of land management. For example, in the five ecological zones exploited (grasslands, woodlands, woodland-grass, chaparral, and coniferous forest), Indians practiced controlled burning. Within the woodland-grass and grassland zones, fires reduced brush cover, which lessened the hazards of wildfires and increased plant and animal productivity. In the chaparral zone, fire, by destroying the upper portions of shrub species, allowed new growth to emerge that attracted browsing animals. Select fires in the woodlands and coniferous forest zones created parklike conditions which gave Indians easy access in their search for plants and animals.[3]

Techniques of land management are also evident in protohorticultural activities. The Ipai, Tipai, Cahuilla, Wintu, Maidu, Miwok, Yokuts, Panamint, Hupa, Yurok, and Karok planted tobacco. The Ipai and Tipai sometimes transplanted wild plants to areas where they could be better tended, and the Cahuilla regularly pruned mesquite to improve growth.

By the first decade of the nineteenth century, some groups in the interior of southern California—the Cahuilla, Ipai, Tipai, and Chemehuevi in particular—were raising corn and other crops. Since agriculture was not well established at the Spanish coastal missions in southern California until the 1770s, it is unlikely that knowledge of crop growing could have diffused eastward in so short a period. Indeed, this period of some thirty years (1770s to early 1800s) must be weighed against the hundreds of years in which knowledge of farming could have spread westward from the Colorado River where horticulture long preceded the arrival of Europeans.[4]

Further evidence of aboriginal horticulture is found in the traditions of the Cahuilla, Ipai, and Tipai. All three peoples possess agricultural motifs in their legends. In the Cahuilla creation myth, for example, Mukat, one of the two creators of the universe, gave his people a gift consisting of all kinds of strange plants. A shaman journeyed to the land of the spirits to learn the meaning of the gift. Mukat told the shaman:

> They are from my body. . . . That big tree is tobacco. It is my heart. It can be cleaned with white clay, and smoked in the big house to drive away evil spirits. The vines with the yellow squashes are from my stomach, watermelons are from the pupil of my eye, corn is from my teeth, wheat is my lice eggs, beans are from my semen, and all other vegetables are from other parts of my body.[5]

It seems, therefore, that a few societies in the interior of southern California farmed selectively and on a limited scale prior to contact with Europeans. But most California Indians found their hunting and gathering economy eminently satisfactory and not in need of significant modification. Not until the Spanish intrusion did food production gradually begin to replace food procurement as the primary means of subsistence.

Intrusion

N O MATTER HOW BRIEF their stay or how limited their numbers, Europeans usually receive the credit for initiating history in the so-called New World. Thus, in many conventional accounts, the arrival of Juan Rodríquez Cabrillo at San Diego in 1542 marks the beginning of California history, even though his command consisted of two tiny ships that plied California waters for only three months. Of course, a long Indian history preceded Cabrillo's landing, and Indians remained the principal agents in the historical process through the following two centuries. During this period, however, some cultural interchange took place as European seamen and coastal and island Indians came into intermittent contact. Indian culture in southern California may have been profoundly affected by this contact, but elsewhere European influence was negligible at best.

After 1769 and the establishment of permanent Spanish settlements, Indian culture came under enormous pressure. But the first Californians did not readily submit to foreign domination as is sometimes thought. Rather, they implemented strategies of evasion, selective acculturation, and military resistance. Indians possessing prior experience with Europeans were better able to assess the intentions of the settlers than were those who had remained outside the contact zones. This experience may account for the open hostility demonstrated by southern California societies shortly after the Spanish arrived.

Initial Contact

UPON FIRST SIGHTING a European sailing vessel, Indians experienced severe shock. One day, literally out of the blue, an object like nothing they had ever seen suddenly appeared on the horizon. To the Kashaya Pomo, this experience was so profound that centuries later it was still recalled. In 1958, Essie Parrish gave an anthropologist this impression:

> In the old days, before the white people came up here, there was a boat sailing on the ocean from the south. Because before that they had never seen a boat, they said, "Our world must be coming to an end. Couldn't we do something? This big bird floating on the ocean is from somewhere, probably from up high. Let us plan a feast. Let us have a dance." They followed its course with their eyes to see what it would do. Having done so, they promised Our Father [a feast] saying that destruction was upon them.
>
> When they had done so, they watched [the ship] sail way up north and disappear.... They were saying that nothing had happened to them—the big bird person had sailed northward without doing anything—because of the promise of a feast.... Consequently they held a feast and a big dance.1

Perhaps the Kashaya Pomo had sighted the vessel of Bartolomé Ferrelo, who had taken command of the Cabrillo expedition after the famous Portuguese seaman died on San Miguel Island in January 1543. Ferrelo reached the southern coast of Oregon before returning to Mexico.

Thirty-seven years elapsed between Cabrillo's visit and the next recorded landing of Europeans in Alta California. In 1579 the *Golden Hind,* captained by Sir Francis Drake, dropped anchor probably in the bay that bears his name, some thirty miles north of the entrance to San Francisco harbor. In *The World Encompassed,* Drake described his first meeting with Coast Miwoks.

> The next day after our comming to anchor in the aforesaid harbour, the people of the countrey shewed themselues; sending off a man with great expedition to vs in a canow. Who being yet but a little from the shoare, and a great way from our ship, spake to vs continually as he came rowing on. And at last at a

reasonable distance staying himselfe, he began more solemnely a long and tedious oration, after his manner: vsing in the deliuerie thereof, many gestures and signes, mouing his hands, turning his head and body many wayes; and after his oration ended, with great shew of reuerence and submission, returned back to shoare againe. He shortly came againe the second time in like manner, and so a third time: When he brought with him (as a present from the rest) a bunch of feathers, much like the feathers of a blacke crow, very neatly and artifically gathered vpon a string, and drawne together into a round bundle; being very cleane and finely cut, and bearing in length an equall proportion one with another; a speciall cognizance (as wee afterwards obserued) which they that guard their kings person, weare on their heads. With this also he brought a little basket made of rushes, and filled with an herb which they called *Tabah*.[2]

The Miwoks and the English exchanged gifts—shirts, linens, and cloth for quivers, feathers, and skins—but Indian culture was barely affected by the Europeans who remained five weeks repairing their ship.

To the south, on Santa Catalina Island, the European impact may have been significant. Documents produced by members of the Sebastián Vizcaíno expedition of 1602 reveal something about Indian-white interaction on the island. During Vizcaíno's five-day visit, Gabrielino Indians witnessed a Mass conducted in a makeshift chapel, and apparently some sought instruction in Catholicism. They also experienced Spanish might. A few soldiers stumbled onto a religious shrine consisting of an altar decorated with eagle feathers and an effigy they identified as a representation of the devil. When two large crows flew from the shrine to a nearby rock, a soldier shot and killed them with his arquebùs. Apparently, the soldiers believed the devil spoke to the Indians through the brds. The Indians present wept openly.[3]

A correlation may exist between Vizcaíno's visit and a phenomenon that has confused California anthropologists for years—namely, the presence of a widespread religion in southern California that had developed by or emerged shortly after the beginning of Spanish colonization in 1769. Called Chinigchinich, the religion professed a universal god who dictated ritual and the conduct of daily life and who punished the disobedient. According to tradition, Chinigchinich told his followers:

> When I die, I shall ascend above, to the stars, and from thence, I shall always see you. To those who have kept my commandments, I shall give all they ask of me; but those who obey not my teachings, nor believe them, I shall punish severely. I will send unto them bears to bite, and serpents to sting them; they shall be without food, and have diseases that they may die.[4]

Evidently, the Gabrielino on Santa Catalina Island or the adjacent mainland created the religion. In one form or another it diffused over much of southern California, superimposing itself over, but not replacing the older spiritual traditions of the region. The Gabrielino and Luiseño were its most ardent believers and practitioners, but the Ipai, Tipai, Cahuilla, Cupeño, and other southern California peoples also accepted its tenets.

Aspects of the religion are so similar to Christianity, especially its universal god, that some anthropologists insist its development was linked to Spanish colonization. Others maintain it was an indigenous creation in existence long before 1769, although they admit being perplexed by its avenging, wrathful deity. Neither theory, however, is altogether convincing. That aspects of Christianity could have diffused over such a vast area immediately after colonization began is unlikely. That the similarities to Christianity are purely coincidental also is difficult to accept. A third possibility exists.

During Vizcaíno's brief stay on Santa Catalina, Indians witnessed Catholic religious ceremonies and sought spiritual information. Additional knowledge could have been acquired from seamen of later expeditions who visited the island or were shipwrecked in neighboring waters. Moreover, the priests assigned to Spanish vessels would not have missed the opportunity to proselytize. The possibility exists, therefore, that during the century and a half between the visit of Vizcaíno and the establishment of the first Spanish mission, a new religion, possessing both Christian and traditional elements, emerged and spread over southern California.

The religion could not have developed solely from intermittent preaching and teaching, however. A corresponding cultural need was necessary. Perhaps the discontent created by the spread of European diseases produced such a need. The susceptibility of Indians to contagious diseases is well documented after 1769, so it is likely that infection had also occurred during the preceding two centuries. Since many of Vizcaíno's men were ill, infection could have come as early as 1602.

If the Indians identified Europeans as the cause of their suffering, they probably sought European spiritual power to combat the evil. Chinigchinich may have been the result, a syncretic religion possessing elements of Christianity and traditional beliefs created to revitalize Indian culture. If this theory holds, the Indians of southern California had adapted successfully to European contact and ideas long before Spanish colonization began. This adaptability would be fully tested after 1769.

Spanish Settlement

HAD THE SPANISH been more realistic in their appraisal of the intentions of rival European powers, the Indians of Alta California would have remained free of white domination for a longer period than was the case. Spain feared that the Russians intended to occupy Alta California and also suspected England of coveting the region. International paranoia, therefore, not religious idealism or the dream of acquiring great wealth, motivated Spain to colonize the region.

The plan to extend the Spanish flag to Alta California originated with José de Gálvez, the *visitador-general*. His task entailed the inspection of Spanish settlements and programs in New Spain and, if warranted, the initiation of new colonial programs. One of his goals became the settlement of Alta California. In 1769 he dispatched four expeditions, two by land and two by sea, from southern Baja California. Joining forces at San Diego, the Spaniards immediately constructed a presidio, or fort, and on July 16 founded Mission San Diego de Alcalá, the first of twenty-one missions eventually established in Alta California. While Father Junípero Serra, leader of the missionaries, remained in San Diego, an exploring party led by Gaspar de Portolá journeyed up the coast to San Francisco Bay. Returning to San Diego where they recuperated and resupplied, Portolá

Costanoans Fighting a Spanish Soldier, ca. 1791. (*Courtesy of Copley Books, San Diego, California*)

and his men marched back up the coast to Monterey to found a mission and a presidio. Thus, in the first year of colonization, the Spanish constructed two missions and two forts.

Because of Alta California's geographical isolation from the rest of Spain's possessions, the establishment of a road linking the new province and Pimería Alta in what is today southern Arizona and northern Sonora became a top priority. In 1774 Juan Bautista de Anza took some thirty volunteers from the presidio at Tubac, near present Tucson, to the Colorado River where he contacted the friendly Quechan Indians. He then crossed the Mohave Desert to the coast. The two provinces had been linked, and the future of Spanish colonization in California looked bright.

Indian discontent, however, was growing in the San Diego region. In early November 1775, perhaps as many as eight hundred Ipai and Tipai, representing some forty villages, surrounded the mission and presidio. Two neophytes, as the Indian converts were called, organized the rebellion because they feared Christianity was undermining their traditional culture. The attack on the presidio was called off, but the Indians killed a padre and two artisans and burned down several buildings at the mission. When the Spanish retaliated by attacking neighboring villages, the leaders of the rebellion escaped into the interior.

The rebels may have been in contact with the Quechans, who had split into anti- and pro-Spanish factions. Olleyquotequiebe, better known as Salvador Palma, led the latter and encouraged the Spanish to settle in Quechan territory. Palma intended to become an ally, not a vassal, of the Spanish, probably to bolster his own political position and to strengthen the military posture of the Quechans vis-à-vis neighboring Indian peoples.

In the fall of 1776, Palma journeyed to Mexico City, and with the assistance of Juan Bautista de Anza wrote a letter to the viceroy that presented practical reasons why the Spanish should settle in his territory.

> My country is abundant in wheat, maize, beans, cotton, tobacco, watermelons, calabashes, and cantaloupes, and is capable, as I see it, of producing many other products, with which the settlements would be able to sustain themselves in plenty. My people number more than three thousand, with whom I obligate myself to defend the missionaries and Spaniards from every insult. I believe that my neighbors will follow my example; and, in case of necessity, I have no doubt I could draw into a general alliance in the services of his Majesty the Galchedunes, Jamajá, or Soyopas, Pimas, Opas, Cocomaricopas, Cajuenes, Jaliquamas, Cucupas, Comeiás, Pápagos, and part of the Apaches who live on the opposite bank of the Colorado River and who do not communicate with those of this other bank, some because of enmity, and others for the fear which my victories have inspired in them. This alliance, together with the establishments in my country, would not only keep the roads secure for the Spaniards, and keep free mutual communications between California and Sonora, San Francisco and New Mexico, because they will be situated in the center of these provinces, but also, aided by the arms of the Spaniards, we could serve to advantage in the pacification of neighboring kingdoms.[5]

Four years later the Spanish established two pueblos near present Yuma, Arizona. They had lost valuable time, however, because the anti-Spanish faction, under Palma's brother, Ygnacio, had recently gained ascendancy. Moreover, the Spanish soon alienated the Quechans by occupying valuable river bottom land and reneging on presents and trade goods. Reversing his position, Palma joined the anti-Spanish faction, and in July 1781 the Quechans struck at the settlements, killing over fifty Spaniards, including four priests, and taking a number of prisoners. The Spanish responded with military expeditions from Mexico that recovered some of the captives. But they were unable to reestablish their settlements on the Colorado and keep open the road linking Pimería Alta and Alta California.

The Quechan uprising was one of the most important Indian resistance movements in the history of the Southwest. It severely hindered Spanish colonization efforts in Alta California because henceforth supplies and settlers had to come by ship or by the difficult overland route through the mountains and deserts of Baja California. By limiting the numbers of Spaniards who settled in Alta California, the uprising benefited the coastal Indians who took the brunt of Spanish colonization. Unfortunately, the coastal peoples, divided into literally hundreds of small-scale, kin-oriented political units, found it impossible to unite in military alliances that could have driven the numerically inferior intruders from their homelands.

CHAPTER THREE

Mission Life

IN THEIR EVALUATIONS of the Spanish missionaries, historians have often emphasized intent and downplayed result. That is to say, they have spent more time investigating the policies and goals of the Franciscans than in analyzing the impact these goals and policies had on the Indian population. The missionaries are thus remembered not for what they achieved but for what they intended to achieve. History has been badly distorted as a result because no matter how great their sacrifice or how noble their cause, the Franciscans sought to alter drastically the lives of the California Indians and introduced enormous suffering in the process.

History has been further distorted by the widespread belief that the Spanish truly dominated the Indian population. They eventually extended control over coastal groups residing between San Francisco and San Diego and defeated and rounded up interior peoples on intermittent military and ecclesiastical expeditions. But they lacked the manpower and the will to extend their authority to far northern and inland peoples. And they were often hard pressed to maintain control over the Indians they brought into the missions.

Discontent

A LTHOUGH A FEW Indian groups displayed open hostility to the Spaniards who settled in their territories, most offered no resistance. Some Indians eagerly sought mission residence because the padres provided them with food and protection from enemies. Others drifted into the missions to acquire the special spiritual powers they believed the missionaries possessed. Indians were also impressed with the practical knowledge and skills the Spanish were willing to impart.

Because each mission was designed to be economically self-sufficient, Indians learned to cultivate wheat, barley, corn, peas, beans, and various other crops. The ease with which they gained horticultural skills probably stemmed from their vast knowledge of wild-food harvesting and processing. Indians were also taught to manufacture bricks, tiles, saddles, candles, soap, and many other items and to perform a variety of domestic tasks, such as weaving and cooking. The special few who became *vaqueros,* or cowboys, were assigned to outlying mission estates to tend the large herds of cattle and horses.

Two resident priests governed each mission. They were assisted by *majordomos,* or overseers, one or two other officers, a few soldiers, and artisans. Together they formed the ruling group at each mission and considered themselves *gente de razón,* or people of reason, although few were true Spaniards. Most descended from Indian-Spanish ancestry. At any one mission, they rarely exceeded thirty souls, while the neophyte population sometimes grew to over a thousand.

Mission social ranking is vividly described by Pablo Tac, a literate neophyte who wrote an account of mission life sometime between 1834 and 1841 while in Rome.

> In the Mission of San Luis Rey de Francia the Fernandino Father is like a king. He has his pages, alcaldes, majordomos, musicians, soldiers. . . . The pages are for him and for the Spanish and Mexican, English and Anglo-American travelers. The alcaldes [are] to help him govern all the people of the Mission. . . . The majordomos are in the distant districts, almost all Spaniards. The

musicians... [assist during] the holy days and all the Sundays
and holidays of the year, with them the singers [; they] are all
Indian neophytes. Soldiers [are present] so that nobody does
injury to Spaniard or to Indian; there are ten of them and they
go on horseback.[1]

The neophyte population at each mission was divided into
three residential groups. Married couples and their young children resided in a village outside the mission walls; girls from
about the age of eight and unmarried women lived in a dormitory called the *monjerío;* and boys and single men occupied
separate quarters. The dormitories also served as training
schools for the young neophytes.

In charge of the girls and young women was a *maestra* who
oversaw their instruction in temporal and spiritual matters. She
locked the dormitory each night from the outside to ensure her
wards remained faithful to Christian morality. The neophytes at
Mission San Buenaventura, however, cleverly overcame this
obstacle. According to Fernando Librado, a Chumash born in
the early nineteenth century,

> the young women would take their silk shawls and tie them
> together with a stone on one end and throw them over the wall.
> This was done so that the Indian boys outside the high adobe
> wall could climb up. The boys would have bones from the
> slaughter house which were nicely cleaned, and they would tie
> them on the shawls so that they could climb these shawls using
> the bones for their toes. . . . The boys would stay in there with
> those girls till the early hours of the morning. Then they would
> leave. They had a fine time sleeping with the girls.[2]

In 1779 the governor of California decreed that the neophytes at each mission elect two *alcaldes,* or magistrates, and two
regidores, or councilmen, from their ranks. The governor wanted
the neophytes to gain governmental experience since each mission was to be secularized (transformed into a self-governing
community) after a period of ten years. The priests, however,
saw to it that only the most acculturated and trusted of the neophytes became alcaldes. Tac stated that the padres "appointed
alcaldes from the people themselves that knew how to speak
Spanish more than the others and were better than the others in

Gambling Game at Mission San Francisco, ca. 1816. (*Reproduced through the courtesy of the Bancroft Library, University of California, Berkeley, California*)

their customs."[3] Because the alcaldes had a vested interest in maintaining the mission system, many abused their authority. In 1892 Lorenzo Asisaro, who had been a neophyte at Santa Cruz, remembered the harsh discipline.

> The Indians at the mission were very severely treated by the padres, often punished by fifty lashes on the bare back. They were governed somewhat in the military style, having sergeants, corporals, and overseers [i.e., alcaldes and regidores] who were Indians, and they reported to the padres any disobedience or infraction of the rules, and then came the lash without mercy, the women the same as the men.[4]

Because of their limited numbers, the gente de razón relied heavily on the alcaldes to keep the neophytes in line. But many Indians resented being governed by persons without a traditional base for their authority and deferred to lineage officials as long as they could. "Even today," reported a padre at San Carlos Borroméo in 1814, "they show more respect and submission to their chiefs than to the *alcaldes* who have been placed over them for their advancement as citizens."[5] At San Luis Rey, shortly after a padre had instructed a neophyte congregation on how to avoid the influence of Satan, a traditional leader responded: "See how this padre cheats us! Who believes that the Devil will leave us by the sign of the cross? If it were to be done by dancing, as authorized by Chinigchinich, he would depart; but that he will do so by the means which he says, I do not believe!"[6] The congregation agreed with the leader.

Father Gerónimo Boscana, who recorded this incident, admitted that Christianity was only superficially adopted by many neophytes. In 1817, at San Juan Capistrano, he witnessed the refusal of a young man, fluent in Spanish and well instructed in Catholicism, to confess and take the sacrament while lying near death. When asked to explain his obstinacy, the Indian retorted: "If I have been deceived whilst living, I do not wish to die in the delusion!" According to Boscana, this kind of defiance was commonplace. "As all their operations are accompanied by stratagems and dissimulation," he confessed, "they easily gain our confidence and at every pass we are deluded."[7]

Death was a common occurrence at the missions. Each experienced one of more epidemics of smallpox, measles, dysentery, pleurisy, pneumonia, and syphilis. The shock at seeing their friends and families die in mysterious and often horrible ways caused some neophytes to renounce Christianity and attempt, at least on one occasion, their own remedy. At Mission Santa Bárbara a religious revitalization movement emerged at the beginning of the nineteenth century. The following account, written by a padre, reveals the nature of the movement as well as Spanish insecurity and vulnerability.

> In the year 1801, when an epidemic of pneumonia . . . caused the death of many pagans and Christians, a single female neophyte succeeded in deceiving the Christian Indians of Santa Barbara. It happened that after a pretended trance she said that Chupu . . . appeared to her and told her that the pagan Indians were to die if they were baptized, and that the same fate was to befall the Christian Indians who would not give alms . . . to Chupu, and who would refuse to wash their heads with a certain water. . . . The news of the revelation spread immediately through all the houses of the Mission; almost all the neophytes, the alcaldes included went to the house of the visionary to present beads and seeds, and to go through the rite of renouncing Christianity. The

particular point of the intrigue, and that which matters, is that the fashion extended to all the Indian settlements of the Channel and of the Sierra, and that the missionaries did not know about it.... For three days we remained ignorant of the event until a neophyte, overcoming his fears, told us what was happening. If the Indian woman had added, that in order to stop the epidemics, it was necessary to kill the missionaries and the soldiers of the guard, the alcaldes and the rest of the natives would have believed it too.... Who would have escaped death, and who would have warned the Presidio, though it is only half a league away? This did not happen, thanks to God, but it is enough that such a thing might have happened.[8]

Certainly, reports like this one indicate that by the beginning of the nineteenth century the mission system was suffering from the strains of neophyte discontent.

Resistance

IN 1810 Mexico rebelled against Spain, the turbulence continuing until the achievement of independence in 1821. There followed a short-lived empire, then the creation of a republic in 1824. After centuries of authoritarian rule, however, the democratic process was difficult to master, and Mexico suffered through periods of strife as those who supported a centralized government clashed with those who favored a federal system. In Mexican California this instability and unrest were reflected in numerous but generally ineffective rebellions against the provincial government.

The neophyte population was deeply affected by the political unrest, and it is no coincidence that the most serious mission uprisings occurred during these troubled times. For some alcaldes, the political chaos provided a long-awaited opportunity. Because they had performed important services in maintaining the mission system yet had never been truly accepted by the gente de razón, the alcaldes may have been the most alienated of all the neophytes. Perhaps the cruelty they had exhibited toward their fellow Indians stemmed from the frustrations they felt at being ultimately rejected by the people they sought to emulate and please.[9] But whatever the cause of their discontent, several alcaldes, drawing upon the leadership experience gained at the missions, violently assailed the authority of the Franciscans and the Mexican government during the second decade of the nineteenth century.

The most serious uprisings occurred among the most heavily colonized Indian people of California—the Chumash—who between 1772 and 1804 had witnessed the establishment of a presidio and five missions in their territories. During and immediately after the Mexican war for independence, the Chumash received harsh treatment from local soldiers. In 1824 a Santa Bárbara neophyte discussed Indian grievances with a padre:

> Now you see . . . this is the sort of justice they show us. We have advised him [the presidio commander] many times about the damage the soldiers cause every year to our gardens, cutting down our wooden fences, treating us badly, robbing us of our watermelons and other fruits we have planted, often beating the old men and women who care for them. . . . But we got nowhere. If the padres notify the commander he pays no attention. If we advise him in person we are called imposters and are told we never tell the truth. . . . We are always working to maintain them for so many years already and this without pay. Now that they should treat us with even greater kindness they act in a worse manner. We are acquainted with those proclamations read at the presidio: "He who steals so many pesos forfeits with his life"; "He who does this or that, will be exiled, etc.". . . Before . . . we had the consolation of knowing that if anybody committed a crime, the case would go to Mexico; that we had a means of defence that would look favorably upon us, but now for whatever small cause, the officials are the ones who are to punish according to their caprice.[10]

In February 1824, the flogging of an Indian by the corporal of the guard at Mission Santa Inés sparked an uprising that spread quickly to the other Chumash missions. The Santa Inés neophytes drove the missionaries and guards into a building at the rear of the church and set fire to several structures. The following day Mexican soldiers retook the mission, but many of the neophytes fled to Mission La Purísima Concepción, where their brethren were also in rebellion. Collectively, they held part of the mission compound for three weeks before cavalry and artillery arrived from Monterey. After a battle lasting two and a half hours, the Indian rebels surrendered. Sixteen neophytes lost their lives and many more were injured. Mexican casualties totaled one dead and two wounded.

The day following the uprising at Santa Inés, neophytes at Mission Santa Bárbara, under the leadership of an alcalde named Andrés, also rebelled. After a short engagement with Mexican troops, Andrés and his followers sacked the mission for supplies and retreated into the nearby foothills where they remained for a week before crossing the mountains to the east. Fearing Andrés would team up with local Yokuts and spearhead a general Indian revolt, the Mexicans sent out two military expeditions, the second persuading most of the neophytes to return to the mission. During the next few months, other Indians straggled in, but some 450 remained in the interior. They settled in the southern end of the San Joaquin Valley, intermarried with local Yokuts, and formed a new society.

Alcaldes also organized resistance movements in northern California. In 1827 one Narciso, an alcalde from Mission San José, fled into the interior with four hundred followers and apparently attempted to bring to his banner neophytes from other missions. The following year Estanislao, another alcalde from San José, left the mission on what was supposedly a routine visit to his people on the Stanislaus River. He refused to return and sent word to the mission that he was rising in revolt. Estanislao recruited neophytes from the missions of Santa Clara, Santa Cruz, and San Juan Bautista. From their stronghold of ditches and stockades on the Stanislaus, Estanislao and his followers struck at inland mission estates, making off with large numbers of horses. The Indians succeeded in defending themselves against several Mexican expeditions until finally overcome. Estanislao fled to Mission San José, threw himself upon the mercy of the resident priest, and was eventually pardoned by the Mexican government. Other resistance leaders, many of them alcaldes, were also active in the interior. The numerous

Mission San Gabriel Arcángel, 1832. (*Courtesy of Copley Books, San Diego, California*)

Mexican probes into the Sacramento and San Joaquin valleys during the 1820s and 1830s are testimony to their existence, although their activities remain sketchy.

By recruiting neophytes to their ranks and defying the Mexican military, Indian resistance leaders damaged the prestige and challenged the rationale of the mission system. Making an even greater contribution to the decline of the missions, however, were the thousands of nameless neophytes who simply fled when conditions became intolerable. Fugitivism, as the problem was termed, plagued the missionaries almost from the beginning. Of the eighty thousand Indians baptized by 1831, perhaps ten percent escaped.[11]

Fugitivism, disease, and a declining mission birth rate produced a drastic reduction in the neophyte population in the 1820s and 1830s. The number of resident neophytes peaked at slightly over twenty-one thousand in 1821, but only sixteen thousand remained in 1834.[12] To save the system, the missionaries needed to tap new population centers, and some consideration was given to establishing a string of inland missions to parallel those along the coast. Lack of financial support and personnel prevented the implementation of these plans. But they would have been to little avail anyway, because political developments in Mexico, over which the padres had no control, brought the mission system to a rather abrupt end.

In August 1833 the Mexican government passed a law secularizing the missions of Alta and Baja California. The legislation required the padres to relinquish secular control over the neophytes and to perform only religious duties until replaced by parish priests. As quickly as possible, the missions were to be converted into pueblos and their lands distributed among the neophytes. The head of each family or adult male over twenty years of age was to receive thirty-three acres of land. Half the livestock, equipment, and seeds of each mission was also to be divided among the Indian residents. Remaining land, animals, and property would become the responsibility of civil administrators who would oversee the missions until secularization was completed.

Most of the land and property designated for the ex-neophytes fell into the hands of the gente de razón. Julio César, an Indian born at Mission San Luis Rey in 1824, witnessed or heard about the illegal activities of a succession of civil administrators.

> When Don Pío Pico left the administration of San Luís Rey he bought Santa Margarita Rancho, paying for it with the same cattle which he had appropriated from the mission. I believe he gave 500 head of cattle for that rancho. After buying Santa Margarita, he took two more ranchos—San Mateo and Las Flores. Don José Estudillo, when he ceased to be administrator, took a rancho, San Jacinto, with cattle and everything, and it was no longer known as belonging to the Indians.
>
> Don José Joaquín Ortega, during his administration, appropriated to himself nearly all the mission cattle, but did not take any of its land. It was said that Señor Ortega left the mission stripped bare, making an end of everything, even to the plates and cups. I was not at the mission when Señor Marron entered as administrator, but I heard that he found scarcely any furniture in the house and that in the storehouses there was nothing at all.[13]

MISSIONS
and
RANCHOS
in
CALIFORNIA

SAN
FRANCISCO

SANTA BARBARA

LOS
ANGELES

SAN DIEGO

🏳 MISSIONS

🦪 RANCHOS

N

0   50
miles

What took place at San Luis Rey was not unusual. During the decade that followed the secularization order, most of the twenty-one missions were dissolved under similar circumstances. A few Indian pueblos were established but existed for only a short time. Most of the lands held earlier by the missions were turned into private estates called ranchos.

CHAPTER FOUR

Aftermath

THE SECULARIZATION of the missions is usually regarded as a watershed in California history because it resulted in the replacement of one Hispanic institution by another—the rancho for the mission. Inherent in this position is the view that Hispanos were the principal actors in the historical drama and those most affected by secularization had no role to play. Indeed, most California historians consider the breakup of the missions the coup de grâce of the neophyte population. Cheated out of their promised lands and driven from the missions, the Indians entered a long twilight of despair and degeneration and ceased to be of importance in California history.

Actually, the dispossessed ex-neophytes contributed much to the history of this period because secularization provided them with several options. They could drift into the Mexican towns in search of domestic or agricultural employment; they could petition the government for land grants; they could seek work on the ranchos; or they could withdraw into the interior with the intent of joining kinsmen or establishing new sociopolitical groups.

Economic Integration

MANY OF THE ex-neophytes sought work in the Mexican pueblos of San José, Villa de Branciforte, and Los Angeles and in the settlements that had emerged near the presidios of San Diego, Santa Bárbara, and Monterey. Richard Henry Dana, who visited California in the mid-1830s, noticed large numbers of Indians in Monterey who

> do all the hard work, two or three being attached to each house; and the poorest persons are able to keep one, at least, for they have only to feed them and give them a small piece of coarse cloth and a belt, for the males; and a coarse gown, without shoes or stockings, for the females.[1]

Similar conditions prevailed in Villa de Branciforte (now known as Santa Cruz), where more than 100 Indians constituted a fourth of the population in 1845.

The largest concentration of Indians, however, lived in Los Angeles. Almost from the time of its founding in 1781, the pueblo relied almost exclusively on Indian labor. In the early years, the gentiles, as the Spanish designated the unconverted, non-mission Indians, formed the labor force, but they worked for the gente de razón only when it did not interfere with their traditional subsistence activities. A military officer noted in 1784 the dependence of Los Angeles on Indian labor and the independence of the Indian laborers. "I feel that only with the aid of the gentiles have... [the settlers] been able to plant the... crops... but as these [Indians] are at present harvesting their abundant wild seeds, they justly refuse with this good reason to lend a hand in digging and weeding."[2]

Occasionally, the pueblo imported neophyte workers from the nearby missions, but until secularization most of the domestic and agricultural labor was performed by the gentiles. In 1830 a census of Los Angeles put the number of Indians at 198 as compared to 764 gente de razón. The census-taker divided the Indians into two classes—"domesticated Indians" and "domesticated heathens," that is, neophytes and gentiles. At this time, the gentiles outnumbered the neophytes 127 to 71. The census-taker also noted that relations between the gentiles and the gente de razón were amicable. "The heathens of the neighborhood," he observed, "who come here and work with the whites, are treated well and live a civilized and quiet life."[3]

By the mid-1830s Los Angeles had become an important agricultural center, the growing of grapes and the producing of wine being the key industries. Although grapes had been grown from the early days, the commercial wine industry began in 1831 when Louis Vignes, originally from Bordeaux, imported cuttings from France. As the grape and other agricultural undertakings expanded, the demand for cheap labor increased. Supplying this demand were ex-neophytes who flocked to the town after secularization. The census of 1836 identified 223 ex-neophytes, as compared to only 32 gentiles. The number increased to 650 by 1844, over 400 coming from the southern missions of San Luis Rey, San Juan Capistrano, and San Diego. In less than a decade, therefore, the number of Indians in Los Angeles tripled.

By the mid-1840s the majority of Indians resided in a village located near the present southeast corner of Commercial and Alameda streets. It was often the scene of drunken brawls and killings, and in 1845 the town council forced the Indians to construct a new settlement across the Los Angeles River. Called Pueblito, it became as crime-ridden as the old site, and in late 1847 American authorities ordered its destruction. Henceforth, Indians were housed on their employers' premises or relocated outside the town in widely separated camps.

So essential were the Indian workers that the common council, as the municipal government was called under American rule, saw to it that they became tightly integrated into the town's economic structure. In 1850 the council issued an ordinance with far-reaching consequences: "When the city has no work in which to employ the chain gang, the Recorder shall, by means of notices conspicuously posted, notify the public that such a number of prisoners will be auctioned off to the highest bidder for private service."[4]

Throughout the 1850s and 1860s, local ranchers and growers assembled at the beginning of the work week to bid on the Indian prisoners. As indicated in a letter written by the administrator of Rancho los Alamitos, the practice became callously routine. He asked his employer to "deputize someone to attend the auction that usually takes place at the prison on Mondays, and buy me five or six Indians."[5] Horace Bell, an early Anglo resident of Los Angeles, described the system in which the Indians were caught.

> The cultivators of the vineyards commenced paying the Indian peons with *aguardiente* [brandy]. . . . The consequence was that on being paid off on Saturday evening, they would meet in great gatherings . . . and pass the night in gambling, drunkenness and debauchery. On Sunday the streets would be crowded from morn till night with Indians, males and females of all ages, from the girl of ten or twelve, to the old man and woman of seventy or eighty. . . .
>
> About sundown the pompous marshal, with his Indian special deputies, who had been kept in jail all day to keep them sober, would drive and drag the herd to a big corral in the rear of Downey Block, where they would sleep away their intoxication, and in the morning they would be exposed for sale, as slaves for the week. Los Angeles had its slave mart, as well as New Orleans and Constantinople—only the slave at Los Angeles was sold fifty-two times a year as long as he lived, which did not generally exceed one, two, or three years, under the new dispensation. They would be sold for a week, and bought up by the vineyard men and others at prices ranging from one to three dollars, one-third of which was to be paid to the peon at the end of the week, which debt, due for well performed labor, would invariably be paid in *aguardiente,* and the Indian would be made happy until the following Monday morning, having passed through another Saturday night and Sunday's saturnalia of debauchery and bestiality. Those thousands of honest, useful people were absolutely destroyed in this way.[6]

Smallpox struck southern California in late 1862, killing hundreds of Indians in the town and county of Los Angeles. Thereafter, the Indian labor force declined rapidly and the local ranchers and grape growers sustained considerable economic loss as a result.

Social Readjustment

I N SOUTHERN CALIFORNIA, a few Indians acquired land
grants from the Mexican government and became, in effect,
rancheros. Since the acquisition of a grant entailed filing a
formal petition containing a description of the land and a *diseño*
(map) of the location, the Indian grantees were usually the most
Hispanicized of the ex-neophytes—literate and acquainted with
Mexican legal procedures.

In 1842 an Indian called Samuel received title to the "1000
Vara Tract" in the San Fernando Valley. On his 177 acres,
Samuel planted oranges, pears, pomegranates, and grapes.
Three years later two other ranchos in the valley were granted
to Indians—Rancho el Escorpión to Urbano, Odón, and
Manuel; and Rancho Encino to Ramón, Francisco, and Roque.
In the San Gabriel Valley, an Indian woman named Victoria
secured title to Huerta de Cuati in 1838. And farther south,
near Mission San Luis Rey, Andreas and José Manuel received
the 2,000-acre Rancho Guajome in 1845. Fifty Indians in
southern California were registered landholders in 1852, although within a few years most had lost their property.

The vast majority of Indians associated with ranchos worked
for Mexicans. In many ways, the rancho was an institution of retreat and readjustment, created during the years of uncertainty
after California became a Mexican province. Ostensibly organized to sell products and turn a profit, the rancho produced little
to sell. The hides and tallow sold to foreign sea merchants were
practically its only exports. In fact, the California rancho was
basically a subsistence institution which produced only enough
to support its Mexican and Indian residents and to display, in
conspicuous and unproductive ways, the wealth and status of its
owner. It did, however, weather the years of political turmoil
that characterized Mexican rule in California.

As the locus of authority, the ranchero was employer, judge,
military leader, and sometimes blood relative to the Indians on
his estate. Unlike the missionary, who had attempted to regulate
the social, religious, and economic lives of the neophytes, the
ranchero was not very concerned about the noneconomic activities of his Indian workers. Families and kin groups remained

intact and community life continued relatively undisturbed. But the ranchero, by paying the Indians in kind and by controlling the land upon which they constructed their villages and raised their crops and animals, relegated them to a dependency position and thus created a class of peons. Indeed, upon the twin foundations of private landownership and peonage was a new social order erected in California.

The economic importance of the Indian peons is clearly explained by a prominent ranchero:

> Many of the rich men of the country had from twenty to sixty Indian servants whom they dressed and fed. . . . Indians tilled our soil, pastured our cattle, sheared our sheep, cut our lumber, built our houses, paddled our boats, made tiles for our homes, ground our grain, slaughtered our cattle, dressed their hides for market, and made our unburnt bricks; while the Indian women made excellent servants, took care of our children, made every one of our meals.[7]

On some ranchos a select number of Indians served exclusively as guards. Their job was to protect the rancho against the incursions of independent Indian groups that found the enormous herds of horses easy and tempting targets. The raiders preferred horses to cattle as a food source because they were easier to drive off. Horses also fulfilled transportation and trade needs. The raids, therefore, had a distinct economic rationale and were not designed to destroy lives and property. Nor were they necessarily undertaken to achieve status or express courage as was the case among many North American Indian peoples.

The ranchos in the vicinity of Monterey, Santa Barbara, Los Angeles, and San Diego were often hit, but those in the San Bernardino Valley were especially vulnerable. Local Indians took their share of the valley's horses, but a band of Utes under the leadership of Walkara, caused the greatest problems. From the early 1840s to the mid-1850s, the Utes annually raided the San Bernardino ranchos. They herded the horses through the Cajon Pass and onto the Mohave Desert, Utah being their destination. Walkara allegedly boasted that the rancheros were allowed to remain in the valley for and by his pleasure.

Indian raiding continued into the 1870s, well after the Americans took over California. Literally thousands of horses, along

Mounted Indian in San Joaquin Valley, 1853. (*Reproduced through the courtesy of the Bancroft Library, University of California, Berkeley, California*)

with cattle, mules, sheep and hogs, went into the Indian larder. By substituting new food sources for those depleted by the establishment of white settlements, many Indians became heavy consumers of meat. This dietary adjustment saved entire villages from starvation.

Political adaptation also took place. At the same time Mexicans were establishing the rancho as an institution of readjustment, Indians, especially those in the interior of southern California, were also reorganizing their lives. Strong, self-made political leaders emerged from the confusion created by the breakup of the missions and established what in some cases amounted to new societies. They organized mission refugees, individuals from shattered lineages, and kinsmen into well-governed political units. By creating order out of chaos, these leaders performed the same service for their followers as the rancheros did for theirs.

The rise of new Indian leaders had begun during the mission period when the padres appointed alcaldes to govern the day-to-day activities of the neophytes and selected prominent lineage headmen to serve in the interior as *capitanes* of mission districts. The duties of the capitán consisted primarily in keeping order and protecting mission property and stock. Mexican officials continued this policy by authorizing inland Indian leaders to capture horse thieves and to recover stolen property.

Hispanic influence, however, does not account solely for the rise of new leaders. Some held traditional political positions in prominent lineages from which they expanded their authority. But unlike the precontact headmen who governed by consensus, the postcontact chiefs ruled by power. They adjudicated disputes among villages under their control, negotiated with white and Indian leaders, and summarily punished lawbreakers.

In the San Bernardino Valley, Cooswootna, better known as Juan Antonio, had become the leader of five Cahuilla lineages by 1844. A short time later, he and his followers moved onto Rancho San Bernardino by invitation of the owners, the Lugo family. Their task was to protect the estate against the incursions of Indian horse raiders, especially Walkara and his band of Utes. But so interdependent were the Cahuillas and the Lugos that the relationship constituted an alliance of equals rather than a simple employer-employee arrangement. And as illustrated by an incident in December 1846, the alliance held up well. Under instructions from the Lugos, Antonio's followers killed in battle about forty Luiseños who shortly before had murdered a group of Mexicans. The slain Mexicans had recently helped defeat an American military force that had invaded California during the Mexican-American War.

When the Lugos sold Rancho San Bernardino to Mormon colonists in late 1851, the Cahuilla chief reestablished his main village in a nearby canyon. By this time, Antonio had greatly expanded his influence and authority, becoming in effect the titular head of all the Cahuilla, who numbered about three thousand. He ruled his people with a firm hand until his death in 1863.

Another powerful chief to emerge in southern California was Antonio Garra. Brought at an early age to Mission San Luis Rey where he had learned to read and write Spanish, Garra returned to his homeland in the Valle de San José after secularization. Using his membership in a prominent lineage as a springboard to power, Garra became the paramount chief of the Cupeño sometime before the mid-1840s.

Numbering about five hundred persons, including many ex-neophytes, the Cupeño resided in two main villages, raised cattle and horses, and grew a variety of crops. They remained out of direct contact with whites until 1844 when a naturalized Mexican, Juan José Warner, originally from Connecticut, received a grant for the valley and immediately appropriated land which the Indians considered theirs. Unlike the Lugos, who employed Cahuillas en masse and treated them well, Warner hired individual Cupeños at a paltry three dollars per month and liberally applied to lash to ensure he got his money's worth.

Causing the Cupeño further concern were the U.S. Army detachments passing through their territory during late 1846 and early 1847. The Mexican-American War had recently broken out and California quickly fell to superior American forces. Less than two years later, the discovery of gold brought hordes of unruly whites into California who expressed little concern or sympathy for the indigenous inhabitants.

By this time the Indian population had declined to approximately 100,000, but many societies had survived the Hispanic occupation of California. Some, such as the Cupeño and Cahuilla, had politically centralized under strong chiefs. None, however, would witness the American annexation without further population decline and the loss of sovereignty.

CHAPTER FIVE

New Pressures

BECAUSE THE American occupation of California lacked uniformity, Indian response varied considerably throughout the region. In the north, the Anglo intrusion was so rapid and intense that Indians had little time to formulate long-range strategies or organize military alliances. Instead, small bands, usually operating independently of one another, attacked mining camps and ranches and often paid a bitter price in return. In the south where the initial American impact was less severe, Indians had more time to assess the intentions of the newcomers and devise systematic policies of cooperation and resistance.

Legally, the Indians of California came under the jurisdiction of the federal government, which attempted to impose its authority through the treaty system. The failure of the United States to live up to its treaty obligations with Indian societies is well known, but in some areas of North America the treaty system guaranteed Indians a land base, curtailed inter-Indian and Indian-white conflicts, and slowed the process of cultural disintegration. In California the opposite held true. The first treaties left many Indians landless, exacerbated Indian-white relations, and accelerated cultural decline.

Indian Miners at Taylorville, 1849. (Reproduced from the original in the Henry E. Huntington Library and Art Gallery, San Marino, California)

Violent Interaction

IN 1848 when gold was discovered in northern California, rancheros in the area quickly transferred their Indian workers from ranching to mining. Moreover, during the first two years of the gold boom, a large part of the independent Indian population of the Sierra foothills, from the Feather to the Merced rivers, engaged in some form of mining activity. A government report of 1848 estimated that more than half of the four thousand miners were Indians. Most worked for whites, but increasing numbers mined on their own.

The arrival of thousands of newcomers from outside California during 1849 dramatically altered relations between Indians and whites in the gold-bearing regions. Whereas the Mexican and Anglo miners of 1848 considered Indians an important economic asset, the forty-niners viewed them as a savage barrier to their own financial advancement. They were outraged that some of their fellow miners could muster large numbers of Indian workers while they had to pan in small groups. Direct economic competition with Indians was outside their experience. To them the Indian was not a worker but a warrior, not an economic unit to be exploited but a physical threat to be eliminated.

To illustrate: in early 1849 a party of Oregonians prospecting on the American River took over a Maidu village and raped several women and shot a number of men who tried to intervene. A short time later, Indians retaliated by killing five miners on the Middle Fork of the American River. The Oregonians, in turn, attacked a village near Weber's Creek where they killed a dozen Indians and captured several more, some being employees of local whites. In Coloma they executed seven of the prisoners. Since no evidence linked the executed Indians with the killing of the five miners, they may have been chosen simply because they were mine workers. Shortly after this incident, Indians began leaving the gold fields, and by the early 1850s few remained.

The cycle of violent escalation that characterized Indian-white interaction in the north is further demonstrated by an incident known as the Clear Lake Massacre. In 1849 Pomo Indians killed two white men, Andrew Kelsey and Charles Stone, who had established a ranch in the Clear Lake area and had abused and even murdered some of their Indian laborers. The following year an army unit confronted the Indians and, to use modern military jargon, engaged in obvious "overkill." According to the San Francisco *Daily Alta California,*

> The troops arrived in the vicinity of the Lake, and came unexpectedly upon a body of Indians numbering between two and three hundred.—They immediately surrounded them and as the Indians raised a shout of defiance and attempted escape, poured in a destructive fire indiscriminately upon men, women, and children. "They fell," says our informant, "as grass before the sweep of the scythe." Little or no resistance was encountered, and the work of butchery was of short duration. The shrieks of the slaughtered victims died away, the roar of muskets . . . ceased, and stretched lifeless upon the sod of their native valley were the bleeding bodies of these Indians.[2]

A similar incident occurred between whites and Tolowa Indians. In 1853 several miners departed from Crescent City to prospect near the vicinity of Smith River. A short time later an Indian appeared in town with the revolver of a miner. A party of whites then attacked a nearby Indian settlement, killing several persons, including the one with the pistol. When a search party returned with the bodies of the miners, the local Indians, fearing further retaliation, fled to a village near the mouth of Smith River. A short time later a company of volunteers surrounded the village while the Indians were holding a dance in their sweat house.

In 1963 a Tolowa by the name of Eddie Richards recalled what he had been told about the incident known as the Burnt Ranch Massacre:

> What I'm telling you now, I didn't see that; that's too far back. They told me. . . . The white people got all around them, around that farm, along that big slough. Most of them got on the other side, and when the Indian come across they get him. The others started in around that house. Every time someone go out, never come back in. People in there began to think, "What's the matter, never come back?". . . They set fire to the house, the Indians' house. You could see them just cutting heads off. They stick them things [knives] into them; pretty soon they pick them up and throw them right into the fire. Some of 'em tried to get away, run down the slough. Soon as they get down there, if they don't get 'em right away, they get 'em from the other side when they come up.[3]

Also causing Indian anguish and hatred were Anglo slave raiders. Because Indian children were in demand as servants and workhands, a new business emerged in the early 1850s that continued for over a decade. Although blatantly illegal, slave raiding was stimulated by "An Act for the Government and Protection of Indians," which the California legislature had approved in April 1850. Section three of the act provided for the indenturing of Indians to whites.

Indians often responded violently to the kidnapping of their children. In 1861 the Indian agent for the Northern District of California commented on the problem.

In the frontier portions of Humboldt and Mendocino counties a band of desperate men have carried on a system of kidnapping for two years past: Indian children were seized and carried into the lower counties and sold into virtual slavery. These crimes against humanity so excited the Indians that they began to retaliate by killing the cattle of the whites. At once an order was issued to chastise the guilty. Under this indefinite order, a company of United States troops, attended by a considerable volunteer force, has been pursuing the poor creatures from one retreat to another. The kidnappers follow at the heels of the soldiers to seize the children when their parents are murdered and sell them to the best advantage.[4]

Between 1852 and 1867, three to four thousand children were taken. Added to these figures must be the hundreds of Indian women who were seized for concubinage and adult men apprehended for field labor. In April 1863 section three of the 1850 act was repealed, probably because the question of slavery was then being decided by the Civil War. The damage had been done, however, and the Indians who had lost their children were left with a lingering bitterness.

Fortunately, Indians in the extreme south of the state were spared the terror that gripped the north, yet southern California witnessed an important Indian resistance movement in 1851. Antonio Garra, the ex-neophyte from Mission San Luis Rey who had become the paramount chief of the Cupeño, formulated plans to drive the Americans from the region. He sought the support of the Cahuilla, Luiseño, Ipai, and Quechan and intended to attack Camp Independence on the Colorado River and the coastal towns of Santa Barbara, Los Angeles, and San Diego. As it turned out, the Indians succeeded only in forcing the U.S. Army to abandon its post on the Colorado, killing four Anglo invalids at one of the Cupeño villages, and burning down the ranch house of Juan José Warner.

The uprising failed because Garra was unable to convince the important Indian leaders of the region that the Americans posed a serious threat to their sovereignty. Most did not realize the danger because the American presence was still limited, and some decided that staying on good terms with the newcomers was in their best interest. One such leader was Juan Antonio of the Cahuilla, who captured Garra and turned him over to the white authorities. Found guilty of treason by a military court martial, Garra died before a firing squad in San Diego in January 1852.[5]

Negotiations

IN AN ATTEMPT to settle the disputes between Indians and Americans, the federal government assigned three commissioners to negotiate treaties with as many Indian societies as could be contacted. Those groups which accepted the treaties would surrender their traditional homelands in exchange for new territories where they would be protected from settlers and instructed in the arts and sciences of American society. The commissioners arrived in January 1851, but they lacked proper financing, local support, and knowledge of the Indian-white situation. Moreover, as developments in and adjacent to the Yosemite Valley serve to illustrate, the activities of the commissioners sometimes intensified rather than solved Indian-white disputes.

In early 1850 James Savage established a trading post and mining camp on the Merced River, some twenty miles from the entrance to the valley. Indians, probably Miwok-speaking Yosemites, attacked the post in the spring but were driven off. Savage withdrew from the area and erected posts on the Mariposa and Fresno rivers. There he gained dominance over local Indians and monopolized the gold trade with Indian and white miners.

It was not long before local Indian leaders realized the danger Savage and the miners posed to Indian sovereignty. A Chowchilla Yokuts, José Rey, attempted to unite various groups to drive the whites from the region. At a meeting with Savage in late 1850, Rey stunned the trader by admitting that war was imminent.

> My people are now ready to begin a war against the white gold diggers. If all the tribes will be as one tribe, and join with us, we

will drive all the white men from our mountains. If all the tribes will go together, the white men will run from us, and leave their property behind them. The tribes who join in with my people will be the first to secure the property of the gold diggers.[6]

Shortly after this meeting, Indians who worked at the Mariposa camp deserted, and the following day the Fresno post was attacked. Indians killed three white men, plundered the store, and drove off horses and mules. Several other attacks occurred in the vicinity, igniting what the Americans called the Mariposa Indian War.

In response to the outbreak, the governor of California authorized the formation of a volunteer military unit. Known as the Mariposa Battalion and commanded by James Savage, it consisted of 200 men and officers. The governor also encouraged the three Indian commissioners to proceed at once to the trouble spot and negotiate with the disaffected groups. They arrived on the Mariposa River in early March and quickly concluded a treaty with six Indian societies. The Indians were given land at the base of the foothills between the Merced and Tuolumne rivers.

The Yosemites and their chief Tenaya, however, failed to attend the conference, and the commissioners ordered the Mariposa Battalion to bring them in. A few days later Savage captured a village on the south fork of the Merced. Indian messengers were dispatched into the Yosemite Valley, and the following day Tenaya appeared alone and convinced Savage that his people would arrive shortly. Tenaya could not understand why his people had to give up their mountain homeland for territory in the San Joaquin Valley.

> My people do not want anything from the "Great Father" you tell me about. The Great Spirit is our father, and he has always supplied us with all we need. We do not want anything from white men. Our women are able to do our work. Go, then; let us remain in the mountains where we were born; where the ashes of our fathers have been given to the winds.... My people do not want to go to the plains. The tribes who go there are some of them very bad. They will make war on my people. We cannot live on the plains with them. Here we can defend ourselves against them.[7]

Although seventy-two Yosemites turned themselves in, on their way to the commissioners' new camp on the Fresno River they escaped and fled back to their mountain fortress. The Yosemites were again apprehended when a second expedition entered the valley in May.

In 1928 María Lebrado, who was still living in the Yosemite Valley, recounted her experiences during these frightful times.

> I was one of the seventy-two Indians that left Yosemite Valley at the insistence of J. D. Savage in March 1851. . . . We travelled to lower country and went into Camp under guard and there were many Indians in and around that Camp who were not our friends. Later we all came back to Yosemite Valley. The white men followed us and we tried to scatter. . . . After we were in camp at Tenaya Lake some of us started back to Yosemite Valley. On the way we met the white soldiers. They took us and others who were still at Tenaya Lake to a camp near El Capitan. As we came down into the Valley we found that all our acorns and our regular camps had been burned by the soldiers. No food had been left for us in Yosemite Valley. We remained in the El Capitan camp just one night. Tenaya was with us and he was marched at the point of a white man's pistol. . . .
>
> On the way to the Madera camp we saw a lake and when the white men marched us to it we thought perhaps we would be drowned. Many questions were asked by the white man. We could not answer all questions. One soldier took a small Indian boy and held him over the lake water by the heels, pretending to drown him. The parents were supposed to answer the question asked by the white men in order that they boy would be saved.[8]

The Yosemites were relocated to territory on the Fresno River, but individually and in small groups they slipped away at the first opportunity. "I remained in the Fresno Camp for twelve days," recalled María Lebrado. "After that I went farther and farther for acorns. Finally, I ran away from camp along with the other Indians and came back to Yosemite Valley."[9]

Their freedom was of short duration. In May 1852, when Indians killed two prospectors in the valley, federal troops rushed in. They captured five Indians wearing the clothes of the miners and executed all on the spot. Tenaya and his people fled east across the Sierra Nevada to the Mono Lake Paiutes.

The Indian commissioners continued their work, eventually

negotiating eighteen treaties with over a hundred Indian societies. They set aside about one-seventh of the state for Indian occupation, a land allotment considered too generous by most whites. Public pressure on the state's U.S. senators caused them to oppose ratification, and in early June 1852 the Senate rejected the treaties. Indians who had given up their homelands in exchange for territories promised in the treaties now had neither.

In the meantime, Congress had established an independent Indian superintendency for California, and Edward F. Beale had been appointed superintendent. Beale had favored ratification of the treaties and now attempted to formulate an Indian policy that would minimize the damage caused by the Senate. Influenced by a report he had commissioned from Benjamin Wilson, an Indian agent in southern California, Beale concluded that a military reservation system would best serve the Indians. In theory, Indians would be persuaded, not forced, to settle on reservations where they would receive seeds, farm animals, and instruction in farming methods. A garrison of soldiers would be stationed at each reservation to maintain order and protect the Indians from unscrupulous whites.

In 1853 Beale established the first reservation near the Tejon Pass in the southern end of the San Joaquin Valley. Located on fertile land with an adequate water supply, the reservation got off to a good start. Early the following year Beale reported that 2000 acres of wheat were under cultivation, that 150 acres of barley and another 150 of corn would soon be planted, and that a nine-mile irrigation ditch had been constructed.

Beale's administrative talents do not in themselves account for Tejón's promising beginning. Already residing in the area were sedentary, agricultural Indians. Called Tulareños by the whites, they constituted a postcontact society consisting of refugees from the Chumash mission revolt of 1824 and local Yokuts. Because they lived in permanent villages and grew Spanish-introduced crops, the Tulareños formed the ideal nucleus for a reservation community.

Problems ensued, however, when nonagricultural peoples from beyond the immediate area were brought to the reservation. Ill at ease in a multitribal setting and unhappy with the regimentation, they fled when the opportunity was right. In

UNRATIFIED
TREATY LANDS
in CALIFORNIA
1851-52

SAN
FRANCISCO

SANTA
BARBARA
LOS
ANGELES

SAN DIEGO

LAND RESERVED
LAND CEDED

N

0   50
miles

1930 a Yokuts named Yoimut recalled what her parents had told her about the reservation.

> My father and mother were at Fresno River Reservation about two or three months. Then some of the soldiers took them to Fort Tejón. A wagon hauled some grub along, but the Indians walked all the way. About fifty Indians went on this trip.
>
> There were soldiers at Fort Tejón. It was not up on the mountains but was on the Tejón Ranch, west of the Head-quarters. My father and mother worked awhile at Fort Tejón, but they did not like it there. None of our people liked it. They all wanted to go back to Tulare Lake.
>
> Lots of the Indians sneaked away in the night. So one night, as soon as it got dark, my father and mother left. They went along the foothills and hid every day until they came to the Kaweah river. Then they came down to Watot Shulul, where Visalia is now.[10]

Since Tejón continued to lose Indians, it was closed in 1864. Three years later only five reservations were functioning—Hoopa Valley, about twenty miles northeast of Eureka; Round Valley, some sixty miles south and slightly east of Hoopa Valley; Smith River, near the Oregon line; and Tule River, some thirty miles north and slightly east of Bakersfield. Of an Indian population that had dropped precipitously to only 34,000, fewer than 3,000 resided on reservations. As a substitute for traditional society, the reservation obviously had failed.

CHAPTER SIX

Deprivation

U PROOTED FROM their homelands and neglected by the federal government, the Indians of California experienced both material and psychological deprivation. As a consequence, many sought supernatural assistance in a last-ditch effort to salvage their culture. They turned to religious specialists who promised a future free from the white man in which they and their resurrected ancestors would live forever in peace and good health. Although unrealistic and even desperate in its goals, the revitalization movement that spread throughout northern and central California in the early 1870s gave its supporters short-term hope and thus helped to bridge the gap between sovereignty and subordination.

Significantly, the majority of Indians in California were much better prepared than those in other western areas to adjust to the loss of sovereignty. Unlike the nomadic, buffalo-hunting peoples of the Great Plains whose adjustment to a sedentary, agricultural existence came with great difficulty, many California Indians had become farmers and stock-raisers long before the Anglo conquest. With proper encouragement and assistance, they might have established self-sufficient and even prosperous agricultural communities on the reservations. Because of white settler opposition, legal entanglements, and governmental equivocation, however, the Indians of California became paupers instead of planters.

Revitalization

I N 1869 at Walker Lake, Nevada, a Paiute claimed he had
visited the spirit land where he was informed that the dead
would soon return. Word spread rapidly, and the Ghost Dance,
as the movement became known, diffused into southern Oregon. The Klamath, Northern Paiute, and Modoc Indians, only
recently confined to the Klamath Reservation, quickly accepted
the doctrine. From Oregon it spread south to the Tule Lake area
in California where about two hundred Modocs under the
leadership of Keintpoos, also known as Captain Jack, were
residing. They had fled from the Klamath Reservation in April
1870.

According to a participant in the Ghost Dance, a shaman
from the Klamath Reservation introduced the doctrine to the
Tule Lake Modocs.

> Doctor George . . . brought the word to Tule Lake at the mouth
> of the Lost River where Captain Jack's people were. He came in
> the winter before the grass began to grow. He said the dead
> would come from the east when the grass was about 8 inches
> high. . . . The deer and the animals were all coming back, too.
> George said the white people would die out and only Indians
> would be on earth. The culture hero [Kemukumps] was to come
> back with the dead. The whites were to burn up and disappear
> without even leaving ashes.[1]

In 1871 the Tule River Modocs were ordered to return to the
Klamath Reservation. They escaped the net of United States
troops, killed seventeen settlers, and entrenched themselves in
the lava beds near Tule Lake. Indian and white leaders held
several conferences before Captain Jack and five other Indians
murdered General Edward R. S. Canby and a clergyman at a
meeting in April 1873. All hope for a peaceful resolution to the
crisis now vanished. The Modocs held off repeated army attacks
before surrendering in June 1873. Of the six Indians tried by a
court martial, four, including Captain Jack, were executed.
Transported to Oklahoma as prisoners of war, the Modocs were
not allowed to return to the Klamath Reservation until 1909.

To what extent the Ghost Dance doctrine influenced the Modocs to undertake armed resistance remains unclear. That religious leaders goaded them into war seems unlikely, but they probably counted on the spiritual power offered by the movement to ensure military success. According to Albert Meacham, Indian superintendent for Oregon, the Modocs believed their resurrected ancestors would assist them in the conflict with the Americans.

Elsewhere in California the Ghost Dance exhibited no signs of antiwhite militancy even though it was obviously created in response to the deprivation caused by the American conquest. In May 1871, on the North Fork of the San Joaquin River, the first dance on the western slope of the Sierra was held. Joijoi and another preacher claimed that the big spotted cat, who was the creator of the first world and brother of Coyote, would soon arrive, bringing with him all the ancestors of those assembled. But only those who remained forbearing and amiable with one another would meet the father. Anyone who failed to heed this message would fall while trying to cross the shaking bridge on the road to the land of the dead and would be eaten by water monsters.

In the fall of 1872 a dance was held in the Eshom Valley attended by four or five hundred Indians. The dance lasted six days and was vividly remembered by Yoimut, the Yokuts whose parents had resided for a time at the Tejón reservation.

> When I was about seventeen years old some Pah-ute Indian Doctors came from across the mountains to the east and talked to our doctors for a long time. They were worried because so many Indians had been dying. Our doctors wanted to stop the dying because they had been blamed for lots of it. . . .
>
> The Pah-ute Indian Doctors said that if we held a big new kind of dance at Eshom Valley we could stop all of the dying and could bring back all of our dead people. So the doctors and our . . . [chief] agreed to help. They called this new dance *Heut Hetwe.* . . .
>
> The Eshom Valley dance was the biggest dance I ever saw. Indians came from everywhere, some from Tule River and Deer Creek, some from Lemoore and some from Kings River. We went horseback from Sulawlahne. It took us two days to go there.

The chiefs who had charge of the dance told us that we must
not get angry or be mean to one another at the dance. We were
to keep dancing all the time. Only the little children could sleep.
If anyone did not dance he would die or turn into a rotten log of
wood. . . .

We danced in a big circle at Eshom Valley. Sometimes every-
body danced at once. We held each other's hands. We moved
them from our shoulders down at each step. We stepped to the
left. After we got tired we just dragged one foot and then the
other. Some carried little baskets of beads and threw them on
the ground as they danced. We danced around and around in the
same place all of the time and made a deep ditch in the ground.
It was a new dance to us. . . .

We had a good time at Eshom Valley but we were sorry we did
not see our dead people. Lots of our people had been dying and
we wanted to see them.[2]

The Ghost Dance movement spread southwards to the Tehachapi Mountains, and dances were held every month at the
most important villages in the San Joaquin Valley and foothills
of the Sierra Nevada. By 1875, however, the movement had
lost its appeal and had pretty much died out. Concerning a
dance held near Farmersville, Yoimut noted: "We danced for
six days and nights there, but never saw any of our dead people.
After that we knew the Indians from across the mountains had
been fooling us. So we did not have any more of those Heut
Hetwe dances to bring back the dead people."[3]

Although the Ghost Dance failed to revitalize Indian societies, it served as an important learning experience. When the
ancestors failed to return, Indians realized other methods must
be found to assure their ethnic and cultural survival. Thus in
1890, a new Ghost Dance made little headway in California.
Instead, it diffused eastward from Nevada to the Great Plains
where it was enthusiastically embraced by Indians only recently
defeated and confined to reservations.

Dispossession

THE GHOST DANCE failed to penetrate the Tehachapi Mountains because Indians in southern California had yet to witness the same degree of deprivation experienced by their brethren to the north and thus had less need to call upon the supernatural. When the movement began, the south was free of reservations, and interior Indians still occupied much of their traditional land.

In 1870 President Ulysses S. Grant established the Pala and San Pasqual Agency in San Diego County for the Luiseño. Unfortunately, Grant's executive order split the Luiseño into factions. Manuelito Cota, a white-appointed chief, favored removal to the reservations. His challenger, Oligario, maintained that the Luiseño should remain on their small tracts because they would be deprived of their land base if the reservations were abolished. Oligario's fears proved to be well founded. The white citizens of San Diego County raised such a storm of protest over the appropriation of valuable land for Indian occupancy that Grant rescinded his order. Not until December 1875 were "permanent" reservations founded in southern California.

Seven years later special Indian agents Helen Hunt Jackson and Abbot Kinney reported on the condition of the Indians in southern California. Depending on where Indians were residing in relation to white settlers, the agents were encouraged or saddened by what they saw. At the Cahuilla reservation, isolated in the San Jacinto Mountains, Indians were doing quite well— farming, raising livestock, and sending out a sheep-shearing band each year to work for local whites. Forty miles to the north at the village of Soboba, however, the Indians faced eviction. Jackson encouraged José Jesús Castillo, grandson of the village headman, to write to Secretary of the Interior Henry M. Teller.

> More than one hundred years ago, my great grandfather, who was chief of his tribe, settled with his people in the San Jacinto valley. The people have always been peaceful, never caring for war, and have welcomed Americans into the valley.
> Some years ago a grant of land was given to the Estudillos by the Mexican Government. The first survey did not take in any of

the land claimed by the Indians; but four years ago a new survey
was made, taking in all the little farms, the stream of water, and
the village. Upon this survey the United States Government
gave a patent. It seems hard for us to be driven from our homes
that we love as much as other people do theirs; and this danger is
at our doors now, for the grant is being divided and the village
and land will be assigned to some of the present owners of the
grant.

And now, dear sir, after this statement of facts, I, for my
people (I ask nothing for myself), appeal to you for help.

Cannot you find some way to right this great wrong done to a
quiet and industrious people?[4]

Legal procedures halted the eviction, and a series of executive
orders, beginning in 1883, established the Soboba Reservation.

Indians in northern California faced similar pressures, though
one small group retained part of its original land base by working the white man's system to its own advantage. The Yokayo
Pomo, who lived on the Russian River in the Ukiah Valley,
claimed land that in 1846 had become part of a Mexican grant.
In 1881 the Yokayo, numbering about 135 persons, scraped
together approximately $800 to make a down payment on 120
acres. By working for local whites and by selling baskets and
crops, the Indians collected enough money to pay off the
$3,700 debt and establish firm title to a small land base.[5]

Other Indians were not so fortunate. They either had to
accept the lands offered to them by the federal government or
take their chances in the non-Indian world. The majority preferred the economic insecurity of an independent existence to
the social problems that reservation life presented. This aver-
sion to reservation life is explained by a Tipai woman, Delfina
Cuero. Rather than associate with strangers, she and her parents
crossed into Mexico early in the twentiety century.

We knew there were people up there living on what you call
reservations. But nobody ever said we could go to a place like
that. In those days when you were with one group, you stick
with that group. You can't go in with another. Most of the
people we knew went down there [Baja California] hunting for
different food and they found a place where no one told them to
move on, so they just stayed there.[6]

Indian Shacks near San Diego, ca. 1900. (*Courtesy of Historical Collection, Title Insurance and Trust Company, San Diego, California*)

Living off the reservations forced some Indians to revert to a hunting and gathering existence. Cuero recalled that after her husband's death she was forced to search for food to feed her children:

> Things got pretty bad. I went out on my own and gathered food. I had been taught all these things about how to gather and prepare wild food. I went out and hunted for wild greens and honey. I took Aurelio and we hunted with his bow and arrows and his rabbit stick. Sometimes we found things. Lots of times we did not and we went hungry. I had to beg for food from neighboring Indians and ranchers. Some neighbors helped me sometimes. I went hungry and my children were hungry. Sometimes for two or three days we found nothing.[7]

Delfina Cuero's account describes well the struggle of a single family. But Indians who had retained a certain amount of corporate unity and who had remained on their ancestral lands also were uprooted. Their problems lay in the legal tangle over land claims. In 1888 the state supreme court ruled that Indians

Removal of the Cupeño, 1902. (*Reproduced from the original in the Henry E. Huntington Library and Art Gallery, San Marino, California*)

whose villages were located on Mexican grants could remain in occupancy, even though they had failed to file for their lands with the United States Claims Commission in the early 1850s. The U.S. Supreme Court overruled the California court the following year, leaving several Indian groups at the mercy of speculators and attorneys who challenged their rights of occupancy.

The Cupeño are a case in point. In 1901 J. Downey Harvey, administrator of Warner's Ranch, sought their eviction from Valle de San José. His attorneys successfully fought the case in the California courts, and the U.S. Supreme Court upheld the decision. The advisory commission formed to find new land for the Indians met with Cupeño leaders in March 1902. Cecilio Blacktooth expressed his sorrow concerning removal.

> We thank you for coming here to talk to us in a way we can understand. It is the first time anyone has done so. You ask us to think what place we like next best to this place where we always live. You see that graveyard over there? There are our fathers

and our grandfathers. You see that Eagle-Nest mountain and that Rabbit-Hole mountain? When God made them He gave us this place. . . . We have always lived here. We would rather die here. Our fathers did. We cannot leave them. Our children born here—how can we go away? If you give us the best place in the world, it is not so good for us as this.[8]

The following year the Cupeño were taken to the Pala Valley, some forty miles to the northwest. Being deprived of their homeland produced hardships and bitterness, but at least the Cupeño received productive land in exchange. Few California Indians could claim as much. Of a population that had declined to about 21,000 in 1910, only 5300 resided on federal land. The majority of Indians lived either on private estates owned by whites or in dismal camps on the outskirts of Anglo settlements where they formed cheap labor pools for farmers and ranchers.

CHAPTER SEVEN

Legalities

S OON AFTER THE annexation of California by the United States, confusion developed over Indian jurisdiction. The sole constitutional responsibility for Indian affairs rested, of course, with the federal government, but the state of California repeatedly challenged this authority, implementing, in effect, its own Indian policy. The U.S. government demonstrated little interest in opposing this interference since it lacked a strong legal foundation upon which to build a durable Indian policy.

Fundamentally, the problem derived from the failure of the U.S. Senate to ratify the treaties of 1851–1852. Ratification would have given the government its rightful authority in the administration of California Indian affairs. But without treaties specifying governmental obligations and without a large Indian land base calling for federal supervision, the United States paid only minimal attention to the legal rights and demands of the Indians of California. Eventually, the Indians got their day in court, but the litigation over the unratified treaties and loss of land continued for more than forty years, and the award granted to each Indian amounted to only a few hundred dollars.

Jurisdiction

T HE TREATY OF Guadalupe Hidalgo, which in 1848 transferred California to the United States, automatically granted American citizenship to Mexicans unless they opted to retain political allegiance to Mexico. Although not mentioned separately in the treaty, California Indians were apparently eligible for U.S. citizenship because they had been granted Mexican citizenship in 1821. California, however, quickly intervened to restrict Indian rights. The state constitution prohibited Indians from voting, serving on juries, and testifying in court against whites. By accepting these provisions in California's constitution when it granted statehood, Congress gave the state unprecedented jurisdiction in the conduct of Indian affairs.

Jurisdictional confusion also extended to education. The responsibility for educating Indians rested with the Bureau of Indian Affairs (BIA), which established schools on reservations throughout the country. But most California Indians did not live on reservations. Was the state of California or the United States responsible for their education? Neither government was sure.

In 1860 the state legislature excluded Indians, blacks, and Asians from public schools, but allowed districts to establish separate schools for nonwhites. After 1874 Indians could attend public institutions only if a separate school was not located in the district where they lived. The legislature abolished the separate school rule in 1880 but reimposed it in 1891. After 1921 Indians residing three miles beyond a BIA school could attend a public institution. In 1935 all restrictions hindering Indian enrollment in public schools were removed.[1]

During the early decades of American rule, few Indians received an education, but by 1909 approximately 2,000 out of 3,700 school-age children attended BIA and public institutions. That year the BIA operated four boarding and eighteen day schools as well as a training school, the Sherman Institute. BIA schools emphasized vocational training and gained notoriety for their harsh discipline and inferior personnel. In 1910 Elsie Allen, a Pomo born near Santa Rosa in 1899, was placed in a government school.

> I had received no education up until I was eleven and it was in that year that I was taken away from my family and sent to Covelo in northeastern Mendocino County, where there was an Indian Reservation with an Indian school. A government agent came to see us and talked my mother into letting me go to that place, which was about 80 miles away from where we lived. . . .
>
> At the Covelo Indian school they placed me in a dormitory

with other Indian girls. At that time I could not yet speak English, and soon found myself unable to follow simple dressing and eating chores of the daily existence because we children were not supposed to speak Indian, a rule of most government Indian schools at that time. . . . They tried to keep me busy by giving me cards that had holes in them through which I was supposed to twist some yarn. It seemed so useless. Worst of all this dormitory was burned down one night, the fire believed to have been started by some older girls who hated the school, and I lost nearly all my clothes that my mother had so carefully packed and sent with me.

We had to move to a boy's dormitory and there I was forced to wear boy's clothes. We were given various duties to do, but it was hard for me to understand and sometimes I was punished when I did them wrong because of lack of understanding the language. . . . My stay at Covelo was not very fruitful because of this language barrier, and I often cried at night with homesickness.[2]

Once Indian parents realized the inferiority of BIA schools, many sought to enroll their children in public institutions. In 1926 a Pomo, Stephen Knight, described the difficulties his people in Mendocino County had in achieving a better education for their children.

We were six years trying to get the [BIA] day school in the Indian village where I lived. We appealed, attended conference after conference, and we never could do anything, until finally . . . through the Catholic Church we appealed to Senator [James D.] Phelan, and he took action and we finally got our day school.

But after sending our children to this day school for a number of years, we came to the conclusion that a Government day school is no place to educate your children. So . . . we went to work and tried to turn the Government day school into a district school, to be supervised by the county school authorities. In this we failed for awhile, but finally we brought suit against the trustees of our school district to take our children into their white school.[3]

The BIA welcomed the enrollment decline in its California schools. For basic economic reasons, it was quite willing to transfer the responsibility for educating California Indians to the state. Several government schools were closed during the 1920s and 1930s.

Changes in federal policy concerning Indian land tenure also led to jurisdictional confusion. In 1871 Congress decided unilaterally that Indian tribes no longer constituted independent nations. Indians were declared wards of the United States who would be granted American citizenship when assimilated into white society. Congress soon realized, however, that many "wards" were more interested in preserving what was left of their traditional cultures than in becoming American citizens. This resistance prompted Washington to intensify its assimilation efforts by passing legislation that sought the termination of those reservations considered most responsible for perpetuating Indian culture.

The General Allotment or Dawes Act of 1887 expressed this principle. It authorized the president to divide the reservations into parcels of land. Eighty acres of agricultural or 160 acres of grazing land would be allotted to the head of each family; a single person over eighteen would receive half this amount. The government would retain title to the land for twenty-five years and then turn it over to the allottee with a patent in fee. Citizenship would be granted at the end of the trust period. Indians who did not live on trust land and who had adopted white culture would become United States citizens.

Although reservations in Oklahoma and in the Great Lakes and Plains states were greatly affected by the legislation, few California reservations were broken up. Their small size and aridity argued against the implementation of the allotment policy. In southern California, for example, only eleven of thirty-one reservations had been allotted by 1928. Few allotments carved from California reservations equaled the size proposed in the act of 1887.

Most allotments in California were created from the public domain and land purchased by the federal government and became known as rancherias (group homesites). By 1924, nearly 2,500 allotments had been issued to Indians no longer associated with particular tribes or attached to reservations. Varying in size from five to a few hundred acres of usually isolated and unproductive land in central and northern California, the rancherias became centers of filth, squalor, and disease.

The legal status of the rancheria Indians was especially difficult to discern. Technically, they were wards of the federal government since they resided on trust land and paid no property taxes. But their economic situation affected their legal status because most worked for whites off the rancherias. In theory, a reservation is a land reserve where Indians, governed by federal laws, live and work. The rancheria, however, served mainly residential functions. By participating in the economic life of California, rancheria Indians became subject to local and state laws. The problem was further complicated in 1917 when the state supreme court declared that Indians living on the rancherias were citizens of the state because they did not belong to particular tribes. Some of the legal confusion was resolved in 1924 when U.S. citizenship was granted to all Indians regardless of residence and degree of acculturation. Automatically, Indians became citizens of the states in which they resided. But the granting of citizenship did not resolve the jurisdictional problem because the BIA still considered Indians residing on trust land as wards of the federal government.

Termination and Compensation

A TURNING POINT in the evolution of Indian legal rights and status came in 1934 with the Indian Reorganization Act, which deviated sharply from the General Allotment Act of 1887. It prohibited further individual allotments, provided for the expansion of reservation lands, and allowed Indians to establish semiautonomous governments on the reservations. The new law also encouraged the manufacture of traditional arts and crafts, permitted the use of Indian language in reservation schools, and called for improved health and educational services.

John Collier, commissioner of Indian Affairs in the Franklin D. Roosevelt administration, formulated this enlightened policy. But Collier was always short of money, and Indians did not always agree with his policies. In southern California, for example, the Mission Indian Federation, founded in 1919 to preserve Indian culture and lobby for Indian rights, opposed Col-

lier's efforts to establish reservation governments because they
would be subject to the approval and control of the BIA. Fearing
the bureau was more interested in extending its authority than
in assisting Indians, the federation fought Collier throughout his
administration.

Whatever the merits of the criticism, Collier was one of the
better commissioners of Indian affairs. After his resignation in
1945, the policy of termination, thought to have been perma-
nently put to rest, awakened from only a temporary slumber. In
the early 1950s, Congress considered legislation designed to
sever relations between the federal government and California
Indians. Public Law 280, enacted in 1953, transferred civil and
criminal jurisdiction over California's reservations and rancherias to the state. House Concurrent Resolution 108, approved
in the same year, proposed to end all federal supervision over
Indians residing in California and several other states.

The state Senate Interim Committee on California Indian
Affairs conducted hearings the following year and quickly discovered that most Indians opposed termination. Nellie Winton,
a Yurok of Smith River Rancheria, summed up Indian senti-
ment in a letter to the committee dated December 9, 1954.

> I do not believe that the Indian people as a whole in the State of
> California are ready for withdrawal of the government super-
> vision as yet. . . .
>
> The Government of the United States has not yet fulfilled its
> obligation to the Indians of California. I believe the Indian
> people are still in need of a better education. The younger
> generation are getting that in the schools today. Most of the
> older people didn't have that opportunity. I still say that we need
> assistance in sending our children to school, to be able to feed,
> clothe and meet their medical care or needs. And we still aren't
> paying taxes for our homes and land. If we had that expense to
> meet, too, we certainly would be at the state welfare's doorstep.[5]

Indian organizations and the state of California, which was
not willing to assume the financial burden of caring for its Indian
residents, vigorously opposed the termination policy. But the
BIA continued to press for separation and convinced many
resident of the rancherias to sign resolutions endorsing a plan
of separation. In 1958 forty-one rancherias voted for termination in which some 1,300 Indians received title in fee to indi-

INDIAN
RESERVATIONS
and
RANCHERIAS
in
CALIFORNIA

SAN
FRANCISCO

SANTA
BARBARA

LOS
ANGELES

SAN DIEGO

• PRESENT (1980)

▲ TERMINATED (since 1958)

N

0   50
miles

vidual allotments totaling 7,601 acres. Upon the request of the Indian occupants, additional trust lands can be removed from federal supervision.

Federal health service to California Indians was also terminated. Throughout the country, the government spend $24.5 million on Indian health care programs in fiscal 1954–1955, the year of termination. California's share amounted to $420,-000. In 1969–1970, the cost of federal Indian health programs in the other states jumped to $99.5 million. Had the service been maintained in California at the 1955 ratio, the state would have received $1.6 million.

Statistics issued in 1962 present an unfavorable record of Indian health in comparison to that of the general California population. The Indian death rate from pneumonia, cirrhosis of the liver, tuberculosis, and congenital malformation was greater than among the population at large; the infant mortality rate was seventy percent higher. Indians could expect to live only forty-two years as compared to sixty-two for Californians in general. With the establishment of the California Indian Demonstration Health Project in 1967, health service for the state's Indians improved, but Indians still contract more respiratory and gastro-intestinal diseases than do non-Indians because of inadequate shelter, sanitation facilities, and diet.

While confronting the problems associated with the termination policy, Indians were also seeking compensation from the federal government for lands their ancestors had lost when California changed from Mexican to American rule. In 1927 the state legislature authorized the attorney general to sue the U.S. government on behalf of the Indians over the unratified treaties of 1851–1852. Claims were filed in 1928, the litigation continuing through the 1930s and into the 1940s. Finally, in December 1944, the U.S. Court of Claims awarded the Indians of California $17.5 million in payment for the land promised in the treaties. The federal government, however, deducted $12 million as money spent for the benefit of the Indians over the years. This left some $5 million to be distributed to individuals who could prove they were descendants of the groups identified in the 1851–1852 treaties. Thirty-six thousand Indians qualified, and in 1950 Congress authorized the payment of $150 per person.

When Congress established the Indian Claims Commission in
1946, Indians sought remuneration for the nearly 92 million
acres not covered in the 1928 case. Approximately 9 million
acres were eliminated from consideration because they had
been officially disposed of by the governments of Spain and
Mexico. The Claims Commission discounted other lands and
reached a compromise with several Indian groups and organizations that 64,425,000 acres were at stake and that $29.1 million
should be awarded. The vote taken among eligible Indians resulted in the compromise being accepted by better than three
to one. With interest and other increments, the award totaled
about $46 million. In 1972 nearly seventy thousand Indians
qualified to receive $668.51 each. Distribution began shortly
afterwards.

While providing some compensation for lands lost, the claims
cases probably soothed the conscience of whites more than they
reduced the bitterness of Indians. In fact, by calling attention to
the crimes of the past, they contributed to the rise of Indian
nationalism during the 1960s and 1970s.

Contemporary Scene

BECAUSE MOST contemporary Indians drive automobiles, watch television, speak English, and live in modern towns and cities, many whites find it difficult to believe Indian culture (except in a few isolated areas) still exists in the United States. Obviously, their perception of Indian culture comes not from personal experience but from cinema and television. Whether depicting them as savage barriers to American progress or heroic defenders of a precious life style, Hollywood has identified Indians as a people of the past. Seldom do we see contemporary Indian life dramatized on the screen.

Indian culture, of course, has changed dramatically over the centuries, but to claim it no longer exists is comparable to saying black culture too is extinct because Afro-Americans are no longer slaves. Especially unfortunate about this misperception is that it prevents whites from understanding the behavior of contemporary Indians. Because this behavior has grown more strident in recent years and in turn has gained the attention of the mass media, non-Indians have been forced to take notice. But the general public probably ascribes Indian anger and militancy to a minority of malcontents rather than to a pervasive discontent that is shared to one degree or another by all Indians. The discontent is real because the pressure on Indians to change has not abated.

Urbanization

UNABLE TO REMAIN isolated from the pressures and attractions of modern American society, many Indians have moved into towns and cities. Whether urbanization is merely the final stage in an assimilation process begun when Europeans first arrived or whether it actually contributes to the preservation of Indian culture by fostering pan-Indianism remains to be seen. But certainly the social and cultural consequences of urban relocation will be as historically significant for Indians as was the earlier removal to the reservations.

Nowhere in the country is Indian urbanization more prevalent than in California. Of a population that had gradually increased to 36,000 in 1951, only 7,168 resided on 117 reservations and rancherias, whereas nearly 11,000 lived in towns and cities. The remainder resided in rural areas and outside the state. Due in part to better living conditions in the urban areas, the population expanded to about 65,000 in 1970. The percentage of those who lived on trust lands decreased further, however.

As of that year, Indians from the Southwest and Plains states had boosted the total Indian population to approximately 90,000. They had come to California either on their own or as part of a relocation plan formulated by the BIA in 1952. Called the Employment Assistance Program, it sought to train and place Indians in jobs near the reservations or relocate them to metropolitan areas. The BIA established employment centers in Chicago, Cleveland, Dallas, Denver, Tulsa, Oklahoma City, Los Angeles, Oakland, and San Jose. During the 1960s some 200,000 Indians moved to these cities.

Urban life has not always led to economic improvement, however. In 1960 Indians had an unemployment rate higher than any ethnic group in California, including Anglos, Hispanos, blacks, Filipinos, Chinese, and Japanese. A fourth of those who found work were employed in manufacturing industries as operatives and craftsmen. Professional or technical occupations accounted for only four percent of the male Indian work force. The high proportion of Indians in unskilled positions is reflected in their 1959 median annual income, which was lower than that for other ethnic groups. Whereas the Anglo male earned $5,109, the Indian male received $2,964.

The unpreparedness of Indians for urban life is also evident in their 1960 educational attainment record. Forty-three percent of men and women had not gone beyond the eighth grade; only Filipinos and Hispanos had a higher percentage. But the poorest college record belonged to the Indians. Only seven percent had completed one or more years of college. The Chinese topped the list with twenty-nine percent.[1]

Indians who migrate to the cities sometimes develop second thoughts. Leaving a rural, kin-oriented community for an impersonal metropolis often produces loneliness and alienation. Those who came from the Southwest and Plains states were often shocked at the spatial dimensions and population size of California cities. In 1973, Jackie Coon, a Sioux from South Dakota, described her feelings upon arriving in Los Angeles.

> This was the first time I'd ever been away from home and, to come out to a big place like this, it scared me. It was way different from what I'd pictured it to be. I felt like I was lost. And like, when I first came, the first thing I wanted to do was go back home. It was just too big for me. That's all. I wanted to go back where it was small. And it seemed like I was all alone out here.[2]

The 1950 census identified 1,671 Indians residing in Los Angeles County. A decade later the number had climbed to 8,109 and by 1970 had reached 24,509. Relocated Indians from Arizona, New Mexico, Oklahoma, and the Dakotas account for most of the increase. Presently, more Indians reside in Los Angeles than in any other metropolitan area in the United States. But no Indian enclave, community, or ghetto exists as is the case with blacks and Chicanos. Indians are widely dispersed throughout the area, although contact is maintained through athletic leagues, clubs, and social centers. Christian churches also serve the metropolitan Indians. In 1968 nine fundamentalist Protestant churches and a Mormon church had predominantly Indian membership.[3]

The San Francisco Bay Area contains the second-largest concentration of urban Indians in the state. The federal census of 1970 put the number of Indians in the seven counties that front the bay at 17,674. Nearby Sacramento, San Joaquin, and Solano counties listed 4,936, bringing the total to well over 22,000. This figure represents a sizable increase from 1950 when approximately 2,500 Indians resided in the ten counties, and is largely a result of the relocation program. Most live in Oakland, San Francisco, and San Jose, where they have established social and athletic organizations and attend several churches that cater to their needs. But they are even more widely dispersed than Indians in the Los Angeles area. It is difficult, therefore, to speak of a Bay Area Indian community.

Though it is relatively easy for urban Indians to pass into white society, few choose to do so. Most prefer to associate and socialize with fellow Indians. A Sioux who had lived in cities all of his life told a researcher in the early 1960s: "Maybe psychologically I am afraid of being rejected; I don't know, but I don't think so. I just don't go to any group that is not Indian. I prefer to be around Indians."[4] This preference accounts for the proliferation and popularity of formal and informal associations and Indian-oriented churches. These organizations serve the communal needs of urban Indians and, in turn, generate a spirit of pan-Indianism.

As a social concept, pan-Indianism emphasizes the commonality of all Indians. It suggests that regardless of tribal membership, place of residence, and degree of acculturation, Indians share the same heritage. Urbanization fosters pan-Indianism because city residence brings together Indians from diverse backgrounds. They learn from one another that intertribal cooperation is necessary if grievances are to be corrected and a heritage preserved.

Activism

URBANIZATION PLAYED a major role in the development of Indian political activism during the 1960s and 1970s. Bumper stickers advertised a rising Indian awareness and militancy with slogans such as "Indians Discovered America," "Custer Had It Coming," and "Kemo Sabe Means Honkey." Floyd

Westerman, a Sioux, and Buffy Saint-Marie, a Cree, wrote and sang songs of anger and protest. Vine Deloria, Jr., a Sioux, issued biting commentary on the mistreatment of Indians in books such as *Custer Died for Your Sins.* Indian militants demanded radical changes in the personnel and policies of the Bureau of Indian Affairs. Most of the activists were urban Indians, and their battle cry, "Red Power," echoed throughout many American cities.

Prior to the occupation of Wounded Knee, South Dakota, in 1973, the most widely publicized demonstration of Indian activism erupted in November 1969 when seventy-eight activists, calling themselves Indians of All Tribes, occupied Alcatraz Island, the abandoned prison in San Francisco Bay. The occupation had both symbolic and practical goals—to draw attention to Indian grievances and to establish an Indian cultural center.

In the treaty language of the past, the occupiers, mainly urban Indians who worked or attended college in the Bay Area, caustically issued a "Proclamation to the Great White Father and to All His People."

> We will give to the inhabitants of this island a portion of that land for their own to be held in trust by the... Bureau of Caucasian Affairs. We will further guide the inhabitants in the proper way of living. We will offer them our religion, our education, our life-ways, in order to help them achieve our level of civilization and thus raise them and all their white brothers up from their savage and unhappy state.[5]

Although the occupation ended when the last of the activists were removed in June 1971, it achieved one of its two goals—wide publicity of Indian demands and problems.

The action taken at Alcatraz stimulated Indian groups throughout the state to implement similar strategies. Thus in June 1970, the Achumawi, or Pit River Indians, took over a campground in Shasta County claimed by the Pacific Gas and Electric Company. Frustrated at the claims settlement that had allotted them less than $700 per person for lands seized from their ancestors, they decided to take matters into their own hands. Of the thirty-eight Indians arrested, most were convicted of trespassing. Each was given a ninety-day suspended sentence, a one-year probation, and a $150 fine.

Not deterred, the Achumawi occupied part of Lassen National Forest in October 1970 and erected a quonset hut. A participant in the occupation, Darryl B. Wilson, explained what
the hut meant to his people.

> They said the quonset hut was "ugly" and that it would have to
> be removed because it "ruined the landscape."
>
> The whole world is rotting. The water is poisoned, the air
> polluted, the politics deformed, the land gutted, the forest pil-
> laged, the shores ruined . . . and the federals spent the best part
> of October trying to tell us the quonset hut was "ugly"!
>
> To us it was beautiful. It was the beginning of our school. The
> meeting place. Home for our homeless. A sanctuary for those
> needing rest. Our church. Our headquarters. Our business of-
> fice. Our symbol of approaching freedom.[6]

On October 27, state and federal authorities violently subdued
the Indians, arresting over thirty. None, however, was con-
victed of a crime.

The occupation of private and government lands was not the
only demonstration of Indian activism during the 1960s and
1970s. Indians also worked within the system. To correct historical stereotypes and publicize Indian problems, Rupert
Costo, a Cahuilla, founded the Indian Historical Society in
1964. The first issue of the society's journal, the *Indian Historian,* contained Costo's publishing philosophy.

> In the past, Indians have had good reason to distrust and even
> scorn the professional researcher. Too often they have misinter-
> preted the Indian history. . . . It becomes necessary now to cor-
> rect the record, to write the history as it should have been writ-
> ten, to interpret correctly the aboriginal past, to report honestly
> the immense contributions to modern society made by Indian
> Americans. . . . Friends of the Indian may join in our great work,
> helping but not leading, aiding but not pushing, taking part but
> not taking over.[7]

From the eight mimeographed pages of the first issue, the
Indian Historian has gained a first-rate reputation as an outlet
for Indian and white poets, writers, and scholars "to correct the
record."

Similar in purpose to the Indian Historical Society is the Malki Museum Association. Founded on the Morongo Reservation near San Bernardino in 1964, the association maintains a small museum open to the public and publishes important books on California Indian culture and history. In conjunction with the Department of Anthropology at the University of California, Riverside, it also publishes the *Journal of California and Great Basin Anthropology*. The first issue of the journal appeared in the spring of 1974 and set a high scholastic standard.

Indians are also taking an active part in public affairs. In 1976 and 1977, Indians in southern California voiced unified and strong opposition to the Sundesert Nuclear Project in several meetings with a committee of the State Energy Resources Conservation and Development Commission. Many were convinced that the proposed transmission lines that would traverse or pass near several reservations represented another attempt by whites to acquire or exploit Indian land. In August 1977, Steven Rios, an Indian who had just been appointed executive secretary of the recently formed Native American Heritage Commission, explained to the committee why Indians opposed further disruption of their lands.

> For three medieval centuries from the 1400's to the 1700's European philosophers and theologians developed elaborate proofs for the existence of God. Indian people needed no elaborate proofs. Rather Indian people simply want their land base, limited as it is, and see the proof for the existence of their God in the undisturbed mountains, woods, lakes and rivers and streams.
> Walt Whitman and Henry David Thoreau shared these spiritual feelings through the concept of pantheism. Their sense of spirit and oneness with the earth came from meditation in an undisturbed environment. Whitman and Thoreau are dead. Indian people are alive. Indian people are fighting today to keep their religion, tradition and heritage alive and intact, so that the Indian land base must be kept free of unwanted intrusions.[8]

Indian opposition contributed to the cancellation of the Sundesert Nuclear Project.

Because their participation in public affairs has also tied up highway construction and land development schemes, Indians are often perceived as blind obstructionists. The validity of this perception is questioned, however, when Indians are viewed as a pressure group, one of many in California attempting to gain or maintain what it considers to be essential. To Indians the preservation of an undisturbed land base is of prime importance to their physical and spiritual well-being. They are applying modern techniques and strategies to achieve this end.

With the conclusion of the 1970s, Indians in California could look to the immediate past with pride and to the distant future with apprehension. They had intensified their efforts to retain what was left of their land base and had regained confidence in themselves. But in the years ahead the pressures to abandon the reservations and rancherias and conform to the values of Anglo-American society will undoubtedly increase.

It is truly an enduring struggle.

NOTES

INTRODUCTION

1. John G. Ames, *Report of Special Agent John G. Ames in Regard to the Conditions of the Mission Indians of California with Recommendations* (Washington, D.C.: Government Printing Office, 1873); Charles Wetmore, *Report of Charles A. Wetmore, Special U. S. Commissioner of Mission Indians of Southern California* (Washington, D.C.: Government Printing Office, 1875); Charles Coffin Painter, *The Condition of Affairs in Indian Territory and California* (Philadelphia: Indian Rights Association, 1888).

2. Helen Hunt Jackson, "The Present Condition of the Mission Indians in Southern California," *Century Magazine*, XXVI (1883), 511–529; Helen Hunt Jackson and Abbot Kinney, *Report on the Condition and Needs of the Mission Indians of California Made by Special Agents Helen Jackson and Abbot Kinney to the Commissioner of Indian Affairs* (Washington, D.C.: Government Printing Office, 1883), also published in *A Century of Dishonor: A Sketch of the United States Government's Dealing with Some of the Indian Tribes* (1881; Boston: Roberts Brothers, 1886); Helen Hunt Jackson, *Ramona* (Boston: Roberts Brothers, 1884).

CHAPTER ONE

1. B. W. Aginsky, ed., "An Indian's Soliloquy," *American Journal of Sociology*, XLVI (1940), 43–44.

2. Tom King, "New Views of California Indian Societies," *Indian Historian*, V (1972), 13–14.

3. Henry T. Lewis, *Patterns of Indian Burning in California: Ecology and Ethnohistory* (Ramona, Calif.: Ballena Press, 1973), 41–80.

4. Lowell John Bean and Harry W. Lawton, "Some Explanations for the Rise of Cultural Complexity in Native California with Comments on Proto-Agriculture and Agriculture," in *ibid.*, v–xlvii.

5. Quoted in Harry W. Lawton, "Agricultural Motifs in Southern California Indian Mythology," *Journal of California Anthropology*, I (1974), 56.

CHAPTER TWO

1. Quoted in Robert L. Oswalt, *Kashaya Texts* (Berkeley and Los Angeles: University of California Press, 1962), 247.

2. Quoted in Robert Heizer, *Elizabethan Caifornia* (Ramona, Calif.: Ballena Press, 1974), 85.

3. Henry R. Wagner, trans., "Spanish Voyages to the Northwest Coast in the Sixteenth Century," Chapter XI, "Father Antonio de la Ascensión's Account of the Voyage of Sebastián Vizcaíno," *California Historical Society Quarterly,* VII (1928), 347–352.

4. Fr. Gerónimo Boscana, *Chinigchinich: A Revised and Annotated Version of Alfred Robinson's Translation of Father Gerónimo Boscana's Historical Account of the Belief, Usages, Customs and Extravagancies of the Indians of this Mission of San Juan Capistrano Called the Acagchemem Tribe,* annotated by John P. Harrington and reprinted with a new preface by William Bright (1846; Banning, Calif: Malki Museum Press, 1978), 34.

5. Salvador Palma to Don Antonio María Bucareli y Ursúa, November 11, 1776, in Herbert Eugene Bolton, trans. and ed., *Anza's California Expeditions* (Berkeley: University of California Press, 1930), V, 375.

CHAPTER THREE

1. Pablo Tac, *Indian Life and Customs at Mission San Luis Rey,* edited and translated by Minna and Gordon Hewes (San Luis Rey: Old Mission, 1958), 20.

2. Travis Hudson, ed., *Breath of the Sun: Life in Early California as Told by a Chumash Indian, Fernando Librado, to John P. Harrington* (Banning, Calif.: Malki Museum Press, 1979), 53.

3. Tac, *Indian Life,* 19.

4. Quoted in E. S. Harrison, *History of Santa Cruz County* (San Francisco: Pacific Press Publishing Company, 1892), 46.

5. Maynard Geiger and Clement W. Meighan, eds. and trans., *As the Padres Saw Them: California Indian Life and Customs as Reported by the Franciscan Missionaries, 1813–1815* (Santa Barbara: Santa Barbara Mission Archive Library, 1976), 126.

6. Fr. Gerónimo Boscana, *Chinigchinich: A Revised and Annotated Versin of Alfred Robinson's Translation of Father Gerónimo Boscana's Historical Account of the Belief, Usages, Customs and Extravagancies of*

the Indians of this Mission of San Juan Capistrano Called the Acagchemem Tribe, annotated by John P. Harrington and reprinted with a new preface by William Bright (1846; Banning, Calif.: Malki Museum Press, 1978), 89.

7. *Ibid.,* 80–81.

8. Robert Heizer, ed., "A California Messianic Movement of 1801 among the Chumash," *American Anthropologist,* XLIII (1941), 128–129.

9. George Harwood Phillips, "Indians and the Breakdown of the Spanish Mission System in California," *Ethnohistory,* XXI (1974), 291–302.

10. Maynard Geiger, ed. and trans., "Fray Antonio Ripoll's Description of the Chumash Revolt at Santa Barbara in 1824," *Southern California Quarterly,* LII (1970), 355.

11. Sherburne F. Cook, *The Conflict between the California Indians and White Civilization* (1943; Berkeley and Los Angeles: University of California Press, 1976), 58–61.

12. J. N. Bowman, "The Resident Neophytes (Existentes) of the California Missions, 1769–1839," *Historical Society of Southern California Quarterly,* XL (1958), 47–48.

13. Julio César, "Recollections of My Youth at San Luis Rey Mission," translated by Nellie Van de Grift Sánchez, *Touring Topics,* XXII (1930), 42.

CHAPTER FOUR

1. Richard Henry Dana, Jr., *Two Years before the Mast* (1840; New York: P. F. Collier & Son Corp., 1909), 82.

2. Quoted in William Marvin Mason, "Fages' Code of Conduct toward Indians, 1787," *Journal of California Anthropology,* II (1975), 94–95.

3. Quoted in George Harwood Phillips, "Indians in Los Angeles, 1781–1875: Economic Integration, Social Disintegration," *Pacific Historical Review,* XLIX (1980), 435.

4. Quoted in *ibid.,* 444.

5. Quoted in *ibid.,* 444–445.

6. Quoted in *ibid.,* 445.

7. Quoted in Sherburne F. Cook, *The Conflict between the Caifornia Indians and White Civilization* (1943; Berkeley and Los Angeles: University of California Press, 1976), 305.

CHAPTER FIVE

1. James J. Rawls, "Gold Diggers: Indian Miners in the California Gold Rush," *California Historical Quarterly,* LV (1976), 28–45.

2. Robert Heizer, ed., *Collected Documents on the Causes and Events in the Bloody Island Massacre of 1850* (University of California Archaeological Research Facility, Berkeley, 1973), 18.

3. Quoted in Richard A. Gould, "Indian and White Versions of 'The Burnt Ranch Massacre': A Study in Comparative Ethnohistory," *Journal of the Folklore Institute,* III (1966), 32.

4. Quoted in Edith V. A. Murphey, ed., "Out of the Past: A True Indian Story Told by Lucy Young, of Round Valley Indian Reservation," *California Historical Society Quarterly,* XX (1941), 362n.

5. George Harwood Phillips, *Chiefs and Challengers: Indian Resistance and Cooperation in Southern California* (Berkeley and Los Angeles: University of California Press, 1975), 71–110.

6. Quoted in Lafayette Houghton Bunnell, *Discovery of the Yosemite in 1851* (1880; Olympic Valley, Calif.: Outbooks, 1977), 19.

7. Quoted in *ibid.,* 42–43.

8. Carl P. Russell, "Interview with Maria Lebrado at Bear Creek" (Feb. 1928), 1–3, manuscript, Yosemite Museum Library.

9. *Ibid.,* 3.

10. Quoted in Frank F. Latta, *Handbook of Yokuts Indians* (2nd ed., Santa Cruz: Bear State Books, 1977), 673.

CHAPTER SIX

1. Quoted in Cora DuBois, "The 1870 Ghost Dance," *Anthropological Records,* III (1939), 10.

2. Quoted in Frank F. Latta, *Handbook of Yokuts Indians* (2nd ed., Santa Cruz: Bear State Books, 1977), 695–700.

3. Quoted in *ibid.,* 700.

4. Quoted in Helen Hunt Jackson, "The Present Condition of the Mission Indians in Southern California," *Century Magazine,* XXVI (1883), 523.

5. Charles Kasch, "The Yokayo Rancheria," *California Historical Society Quarterly*, XXVI (1947), 209–215.

6. Florence Shipek, ed., *The Autobiography of Delfina Cuero* (1968; Banning, Calif.: Malki Museum Press, 1970), 26.

7. *Ibid.*, 60.

8. Quoted in W. W. Robinson, *Land in California* (Berkeley: University of California Press, 1948), 21.

CHAPTER SEVEN

1. Ferdinand F. Fernández, "Except a California Indian: A Study in Legal Discrimination," *Southern California Quarterly*, L (1968), 167–168.

2. Elsie Allen, *Pomo Basketmaking: A Supreme Art for the Weaver* (Healdsburg, Calif.: Naturegraph Publishers, 1972), 10–11.

3. Quoted in "Indians in California," *Transactions of the Commonwealth Club of California*, XXI (1926), 142.

4. Imre Sutton, "Private Property in Land among Reservation Indians in Southern California," in *Association of Pacific Coast Geographers Yearbook*, XXIX (1967), 77.

5. Quoted in *Progress Report to the Legislature by the Senate Interim Committee on California Indian Affairs* (Sacramento: State Printing Office, n.d.), 216.

6. Omer C. Stewart, "Litigation and Its Effects," in Robert Heizer, ed., *Handbook of North American Indians*, Vol. VIII: *California* (Washington, D.C.: Smithsonian Institution, 1978), 705–713.

CHAPTER EIGHT

1. "American Indians in California" (San Francisco: Fair Employment Practice Commission, 1965), 10–13.

2. Quoted in Dan Blackburn, "The Urban Indian: Lost Alone, Longing for Home," *Long Beach Independent Press Telegram*, October 21, 1973.

3. John A. Price, "The Migration and Adaptation of American Indians to Los Angeles, *Human Organization*, XXVII (1968), 168–177.

4. Quoted in Joan Ablon, "Relocated American Indians in the San Francisco Bay Area," *Human Organization*, XXIII (1964), 303.

5. Quoted in Robert C. Day, "The Emergence of Activism as a Social Movement," in Howard M. Bahr, Bruce A. Chadwick, and Robert C. Day, eds., *Native Americans Today: Sociological Perspectives* (New York: Harper & Row, 1972), 527.

6. Darryl B. Wilson, "The Pit River Challenge," in Council on Inter-racial Books for Children, *Chroniclas of American Indian Protest* (Greenwich, Conn.: Fawcett Publications, 1971), 323.

7. Reprinted in the *Indian Historian,* III (1970), 67.

8. California State Energy Resources Conservation and Development Commission, *Hearings in the Matter of Intention for Sundesert Nuclear Project* (Docket No. 76-NOI-2, August 1977), 13232–13233.

SUGGESTED READINGS

CALIFORNIA INDIANS are the subject of a voluminous literature, and the publications identified here represent only the tip of the iceberg. They are divided into four categories—bibliographies, anthropological monographs and anthologies, published historical documents, and historical books and monographs. Lack of space prevents inclusion of historical and anthropological articles not contained in anthologies, although many of the most important are identified in the notes to each chapter.

Bibliographies

The best bibliography for the novice is Robert Heizer, *The Indians of California: A Critical Bibliography* (Bloomington: Indiana University Press, 1976). Although emphasizing the anthropological literature, Heizer has included most but not all of the important historical studies. A more extensive bibliography is Robert Heizer and Albert B. Elsasser with the collaboration of James C. Bard, Edward Castillo, and Karen Nissen, *A Bibliography of California Indians: Archaeology, Ethnology, Indian History* (New York and London: Garland Publishing, 1977). As the title suggests, this guide includes both anthropological and historical sources. Of special interest is a list of writings by Indians. Those intending to conduct research on California Indians should consult Lowell John Bean and Sylvia Brakke Vane, *California Indians: Primary Resources* (Socorro, New Mexico: Ballena press, 1977). This valuable work lists collections of manuscripts, artifacts, documents, and illustrations.

Anthropological Monographs and Anthologies

For over fifty years Alfred L. Kroeber's *Handbook of the California Indians* (Berkeley: University of California Press, 1925) remained the standard reference work. Although still an important source, it has been superseded by Robert Heizer, ed., *Handbook of North American Indians,* Vol. VIII: *California* (Washington, D.C.: Smithsonian Institution, 1978). Containing chapters by archaeologists, anthropologists, historians, linguists, and other scholars, it synthesizes much of what is presently known about California Indian culture and history. Also of considerable value is Robert Heizer and Albert B. Elsasser, *The Natural World of the California Indians* (Berkeley and Los Angeles: University of California Press, 1980). Complementing these works are two anthologies—Robert Heizer and M. A. Whipple, eds., *The California Indians: A Source Book* (2nd ed., Berkeley and Los Angeles: University of California Press, 1971); and Lowell John Bean and Thomas C. Blackburn, eds., *Native Californians: A Theoretical Retrospective* (Ramona, Calif.: Ballena Press, 1976).

Published Documents

The historical documentation pertaining to California Indians is extensive, but much of it lies buried in diaries, journals, reports, and newspapers. A few important documents have been published, however. One of the most valuable is Fr. Gerónimo Boscana, *Chinigchinich: A Revised and Annotated Version of Alfred Robinson's Translation of Father Gerónimo Boscana's Historical Account of the Belief, Usages, Customs and Extravagancies of the Indians of this Mission of San Juan Capistrano Called the Acagchemem Tribe,* annotated by John P. Harrington and reprinted with a new preface by William Bright (1846; Banning, Calif.: Malki Museum Press, 1978). Written in the 1830s, it describes the traditions and religious practices of Indians of the southern coast and presents a vivid picture of Indian resistance to Spanish acculturation efforts. Complementing Boscana's study is Robert

Heizer, ed., *The Indians of Los Angeles County: Hugo Reid's Letters of 1852* (Highland Park, Calif.: Southwest Museum, 1968). These letters were written by a Scottish immigrant married to a Gabrielino and were first published in the *Los Angeles Star* in 1852. They detail the early beliefs and later struggles of the Gabrielino. Also produced in 1852 was a report by Benjamin D. Wilson for the California Superintendent of Indian Affairs. It contains important information on the condition of the Indians of southern California and formulates a comprehensive reservation policy. The report has been published as John W. Caughey, ed., *The Indians of Southern California in 1852: The B. D. Wilson Report and a Selection of Contemporary Comment* (San Marino: Huntington Library, 1952).

Several collections of documents are also worthy of examination. Perhaps the most valuable is Maynard Geiger and Clement W. Meighan, eds., *As the Padres Saw Them: California Indian Life and Customs as Reported by the Franciscan Missionaries, 1813– 1815* (Santa Barbara: Santa Barbara Mission Archive Library, 1976). The volume consists of a series of reports written by Franciscans on the Indians in their respective missions. Each report contains ethnographic data and some information on Indian response to missionization. Indian-American relations are dealt with in four volumes of documents edited by Robert Heizer: *The Destruction of California Indians* (Santa Barbara and Salt Lake City: Peregrine Smith, 1974); *They Were Only Diggers: A Collection of Articles from California Newspapers, 1851–1866, on Indian and White Relations* (Ramona, Calif.: Ballena Press, 1974); *Collected Documents on the Causes and Events in the Bloody Island Massacre of 1850* (University of California Archaeological Research Facility, Berkeley, 1973); and *Federal Concern about Conditions of California Indians, 1853–1913: Eight Documents* (Socorro, New Mexico: Ballena Press, 1979).

Of special interest are documents written or dictated by Indians. The most valuable is Pablo Tac, *Indian Life and Customs at Mission San Luis Rey* (San Luis Rey: Old Mission, 1958). Tac's brief account is unique because it was written by a neophyte only a short time after his mission residence. Most neophyte reminiscences were dictated to whites long after the events they recounted had transpired. See Travis Hudson, ed., *Breath of the Sun: Life in Early California as Told by a Chumash*

Indian, Fernando Librado, to John P. Harrington (Banning, Calif.:
Malki Museum Press, 1980); Lorenzo Asisaro, "Personal Nar-
rative of a Former Neophyte Born at Santa Cruz Mission in
1819," in E. S. Harrison, *History of Santa Cruz County* (San
Francisco: California Pacific Press Publishing Co., 1892), 45–
48; and Julio César, "Recollections of My Youth at San Luis
Rey Mission," translated by Nellie Van de Grift Sánchez, *Touring Topics*, XXII (November 1930), 42–43. A few Indian narra-
tives of the post-mission period also exist. Especially recommended are Florence Shipek, ed., *Autobiography of Delfina Cuero*
(1968; Banning, Calif.: Malki Museum Press, 1970); and "Pah-
mit's Story" and "The Last Chunut," in Frank F. Latta, *Handbook
of the Yokuts Indians* (2nd ed., Santa Cruz, Calif.: Bear State
Books, 1977), 657–730.

Historical Books and Monographs

Some of the best work on California Indian history appeared in
1943 when Sherburne F. Cook published three monographs in
volumes XXI, XXII, and XXIII of *Ibero-Americana*. Collectively
republished as *The Conflict between the California Indian and
White Civilization* (Berkeley and Los Angeles: University of
California Press, 1976), they examine Indian responses to the
Spanish intrusion, the physical and demographic reaction of non-
mission Indians during the Spanish and Mexican occupations,
and the struggle against the Americans. Only when Cook makes
biological analogies do the monographs show their age. Other-
wise, they exhibit the dedicated research and profound insights
of a scholar far ahead of his time. The only other book-length
work that encompasses the entire spectrum of Indian-white
interaction is Jack Forbes, *The Indians of California and Nevada*
(Healdsburg, Calif.: Naturegraph Publishers, 1969). Although
the work succinctly presents the Indian viewpoint in California
history, the inclusion of Nevada Indian history created problems of balance and unity.

The majority of books and monographs on California Indian
history examine specific topics or themes. The best known is
Theodora Kroeber, *Ishi in Two Worlds* (Berkeley and Los Angeles: University of California Press, 1961), a sensitive account of

a Yahi who emerged from the forests of northern California in 1911. Although concerned mainly with Ishi's life in white society, the book also recounts the tragic confrontation between the Yahi and Americans. Indian reaction to American colonialism in northern California is also treated in Amelia Susman, *The Round Valley Indians of California* (University of California Research Facility, Berkeley, 1976); and Virginia P. Miller, *Ukomno'M: The Yuki Indians of Northern California* (Socorro, New Mexico: Ballena Press, 1979). Concerned with Indian response to white pressure in southern California is George H. Phillips, *Chiefs and Challengers: Indian Resistance and Cooperation in Southern California* (Berkeley and Los Angeles: University of California Press, 1975). It examines the rise of new political leaders among the Cahuilla, Cupeño, and Luiseño and analyzes the policies they implemented towards Mexicans, Americans, and one another. Jack Forbes, *Warriors of the Colorado: The Yumas of the Quechan Nation and Their Neighbors* (Norman: University of Oklahoma Press, 1965) also investigates Indian activities in southern California. The book traces the rise of the Quechans and points out the importance of their resistance in the early history of the Spanish Southwest. Southern California is the scene of W. W. Robinson, *The Indians of Los Angeles: Story of the Liquidation of a People* (Los Angeles: Dawson's Book Shop, 1952). The title explains all.

On federal Indian policy and administration in California, the recommended works are Kenneth Johnson, *K-34 or the Indians of California vs. the United States* (Los Angeles: Dawson's Book Shop, 1966); and George E. Anderson, W. H. Ellison, and Robert Heizer, *Treaty Making and Treaty Rejection by the Federal Government in California, 1850–1852* (Socorro, New Mexico: Ballena Press, 1978). See also the relevant chapters in Edward Everett Dale, *The Indians of the Southwest: A Century of Development under the United States* (Norman: University of Oklahoma Press, 1949); and Robert Heizer and Alan F. Almquist, *The Other Californians: Prejudice and Discrimination under Spain, Mexico, and the United States to 1920* (Berkeley and Los Angeles: University of California Press, 1971).

Most of the publications mentioned can be found in university and public libraries throughout the state of California.

INDEX

Achumawi, 75–76
Alcaldes, 23–24, 26–27, 28–29, 39
Alcatraz Island, occupation of, 75
Algic language family, 6
Allen, Elsie, 63–64
Andreas, 37
Andrés, 28
Antonio, Juan, 40, 46
Anza, Juan Bautista de, 18, 19
Asisaro, Lorenzo, 24

Bancroft, Hubert Howe, 2
Band organization, 6–7
Bartolomé, Ferrelo, 14
Beale, Edward F., 50
Bell, Horace, 36
Bering Strait, 5
Blacktooth, Cecilio, 60–61
Boscana, Gerónimo, 25
Bureau of Indian Affairs: relocation program, 72–74; schools, 63–64
Burnt Ranch Massacre, 45

Cabrillo, Juan Rodríguez, 13, 14
Cahuilla, 11, 12, 16, 40, 41, 46, 76
Cahuilla Reservation, 57
Cajon Pass, 38
California Indian Demonstration Health Project, 69
Camp Independence, 46
Canby, Edward R. S., 54
Capitanes, 39–40
Captain Jack, 54
Cascades Mountains, 3, 6
Castillo, José Jesús, 57–58
Century Magazine, 1
Century of Dishonor, A, 1
César, Julio, 30
Channel Islsands, 5, 10
Chemehuevi, 11
Chinigchinich, 15–17
Chumash, 8–9, 23, 27–28, 50
Civil War, 46
Clan organization, 8
Clear Lake Massacre, 44
Coast Range Mountains, 5
Collier, John, 66–67

Colorado River, 11, 18
Coon, Jackie, 73
Cooswootna. See Antonio, Juan.
Costo, Rupert, 76
Cota, Manuelito, 57
Cuero, Delfina, 58–59
Cupeño, 16, 40–41, 46, 60–61
Custer Died for Your Sins, 75

Daily Alta California, 44
Dana, Richard Henry, 34
Dawes Act. See General Allotment Act
Deloria, Vine, Jr., 75
Drake, Sir Francis, 14

El Escorpión Rancho, 37
Employment Assistance Program, 72
Encino Rancho, 37
Eshom Valley, 55–56
Estanislao, 28

Forbes, Alexander, 2
Francisco, 37

Gabrielino, 8–9, 15–16
Gálvez, José de, 17
Garra, Antonio, 40, 46–47
General Allotment Act, 65
Ghost Dance, 54–56, 57
Golden Hind, 14
Grant, Ulysses S., 57
Guajome Rancho, 37

Harvey, J. Downey, 60
Hittell, Theodore H., 2
Hokan language family, 6, 8
Hoopa Valley Reservation, 52
House Concurrent Resolution 108, 67
Huerta de Cuati Rancho, 37
Hupa, 11

Indian Claims Commission, 70
Indian Historian, 76
Indian Historical Society, 76
Indian Reorganization Act, 66–67
Indians of All Tribes, 75
Ipai, 11, 16, 18, 46

Jackson, Helen Hunt, 1, 57
Joijoi, 55
Journal of California and Great Basin Anthropology, 77

Karok, 11
Keintpoos. *See* Captain Jack.
Kelsey, Andrew, 44
Kinney, Abbot, 57
Klamath, 54
Klamath Reservation, 54
Knight, Stephen, 64
Kwakiutl, 9

La Purísima Concepción Mission, 28
Lassen National Forest, occupation of, 76
Lebrado, María, 49
Librado, Fernando, 23
Lineage organization, 6–7
Los Alamitos Rancho, 35
Los Angeles Pueblo, 30, 34–36, 38, 46; city, 72, 73, 74
Lugo family, 40, 41
Luiseño, 16, 40, 46, 57

Maidu, 11, 44
Malki Museum Association, 77
Manuel, 37
Manuel, José, 37
Mariposa Battalion, 48
Mariposa Indian War, 48–49
Meacham, Albert, 55
Mexican-American War, 41
Mission Indian Federation, 66–67
Miwok, 11, 14–15, 47
Modoc, 54–55
Mohave Desert, 38
Monterey Presidio and Pueblo, 18, 34, 38
Morongo Reservation, 77
Mukat, 11

Na-Dene language family, 6
Narciso, 28
Native American Heritage Commission, 77

Odón, 37
Oligario, 57
Olleyquotequiebe. *See* Palma, Salvador.
1000 Vara Tract, 37
Oregon, 14, 52, 54 55

Pacific Gas and Electric Company, 75
Paiute, 49, 54, 55
Pala and San Pasqual Agency, 57

Pala Valley, 61
Palma, Salvador, 19–20
Panamint, 11
Pan-Indianism, 72, 74
Parrish, Essie, 14
Penutian language family, 6
Pimería Alta, 18, 20
Pit River Indians. *See* Achumawi.
Pleistocene, 5
Pomo, 14, 44, 58, 63, 64
Portolá, Gaspar de, 17–18
Public Law 280, 67
Pueblito, 35

Quechan, 18–20, 46

Ramón, 37
Ramona, 1
Rancherias, 65–66, 67, 72
Rey, José, 47–48
Richards, Eddie, 45
Rios, Steven, 77
Roosevelt, Franklin D., 66
Roque, 37
Round Valley Reservation, 52

Sacramento Valley, 29
Saint-Marie, Buffy, 75
Samuel, 37
San Bernardino Rancho, 40
San Bernardino Valley, 38, 40
San Buenaventura Mission, 23
San Carlos Borroméo Mission, 24
San Diego de Alcalá Mission, 17–19, 35
San Diego Presidio and Pueblo, 17–18, 34, 38, 46
San Fernando Valley, 37
San Francisco Bay Area, 73–74
San Gabriel Valley, 37
San Jacinto Mountains, 57
San Joaquin Valley, 5, 28, 29, 49, 50, 56
San José Mission, 28
San José Pueblo, 34; city, 72, 74
San Juan Bautista Mission, 28
San Juan Capistrano Mission, 25, 35
San Luis Rey Mission, 24–25, 30, 32, 35, 37
San Miguel Island, 14
Santa Barbara Coast and Channel, 5, 10
Santa Bárbara Mission, 25–26, 27, 28
Santa Bárbara Presidio and Pueblo, 34
Santa Barbara, city, 38, 46
Santa Catalina Island, 15–16
Santa Clara Mission, 28
Santa Cruz Mission, 24, 28
Santa Cruz Pueblo. *See* Villa de Branciforte.

Santa Inés Mission, 27–28
Savage, James, 47–49
Secularization of the missions, 30–32, 33
Senate Interim Committee on California Indian Affairs, 67
Serra, Junípero, 17
Sherman Institute, 63
Sierra Nevada, 3, 5, 55, 56
Smith River Reservation, 52
Soboba Village and Reservation, 57–58
Sonora, 18
State Energy Resources Conservation and Development Commission, 77
Stone, Charles, 44
Sundesert Nuclear Project, 77

Tac, Pablo, 22–24
Tehachapi Mountains, 56, 57
Tejon Pass, 50
Tejón Reservation, 50–52, 55
Teller, Henry M., 57
Tenaya, 48–49
Tipai, 11, 16, 18, 58
Tlingit, 9
Tolowa, 45
Town organization, 8–9
Treaty of Guadalupe Hidalgo, 62
Tubac Presidio, 18
Tulareño, 50
Tule Lake, 54
Tule River Reservation, 52

United States Claims Commission, 60
United States Court of Claims, 69
United States Supreme Court, 60
University of California, Riverside, 77
Urbano, 37
Ute, 38
Uto-Aztecan language family, 6, 8

Valle de San José, 40–41, 60
Victoria, 37
Vignes, Louis, 35
Villa de Branciforte, 34
Visitador-general. See Gálvez, José de.
Vizcaíno, Sebastián, 15–17

Walkara, 38, 40
Walker Lake, 54
Warner, Juan José, 41, 46
Westerman, Floyd, 75
Wilson, Darryl B., 76
Winton, Nellie, 67
Wintu, 11
World Encompassed, The, 14–15
Wounded Knee, occupation of, 75

Ygnacio, 19
Yoimut, 52, 55–56
Yokuts, 11, 28, 47, 50, 52, 55
Yosemite, 47–49
Yosemite Valley, 47–49
Yurok, 11, 67